SOLVING LIFE'S PROBLEMS

SOLVING LIFE'S PROBLEMS

by
Dr. Paul Yonggi Cho

Logos International
Plainfield, New Jersey

To my dear wife who has been my faithful help in the ministry.

Contents

SOLVING LIFE'S PROBLEMS

1

Learning the Language of Faith

Faith is of central importance to solving life's problems, for you and I were created to be filled with faith. When we are filled with God's faith we are well on the way to becoming the people God intended us to be. However, when we block and hinder the flow and growth of faith in our lives, spiritual and personal frustration follow. This blockage enlarges any other problems we have.

Faith's Functions

Faith—confident, God-given assurance—functions three ways in the believer's life. Knowledge of Jesus and God's Word forms the basis for a commitment to Christ. But it is with faith that we begin our new life in Christ. This is the faith of entrance into the Christian walk.

But to simply walk through faith's doorway is not

enough. We must also learn to develop our Christian lives. Immature Christians never dare to learn the adventure of deeper Christian living. The mature Christian life requires that faith develop, because a genuine depth in faith leads to a deeper walk with Christ. This is the second type of faith, the faith of development.

Thirdly, it is only through faith that we can receive miracles. One does not have to explore far before realizing that ours is a world filled with needs. Through faith we can release God's power to meet those needs. This is the faith for miracles.

Hundreds of people, sensing the importance of faith, have approached me with the question: "How do I increase my faith?"

This question is of concern to all thinking Christians, for genuine people of God are genuine people of faith. But we are impatient; we want our faith enlarged right now. We are irresponsible; we want God to bring the increase, and not have to cooperate with Him in any changes that must result. We are ignorant; we desire to further enter the world of faith without learning its language.

The Importance of Language

Language allows us to communicate. It is a channel for thoughts, ideas and feelings. Language also shapes our lives, affecting the way we think and behave.

Faith and language are closely linked: "For it is by

believing in his heart that a man becomes right with God; and with his mouth he tells others of his faith, confirming his salvation" (Rom. 10:10, TLB). The words of language confirm the validity of a man's faith.

Continuous confession of faith in God's Word is the basis for the language of faith, a language that must be spoken daily in our lives. Practiced properly in sincerity this language can bring forth a miraculous change in our lives. This language can prompt others to commit themselves to Christ, it can develop our own spiritual lives, and it can release God's power to bring forth miracles.

One of the clearest examples of the language of faith in operation can be seen in Psalm 23, a song of David, the shepherd-king. Through studying this psalm we can begin to better learn the language of faith, a language that is to be expressed during times of normalcy, during times of danger, and in the sight of enemies.

During Times of Normalcy

There is a saying in the army that every soldier fighting in a foxhole believes in God. But faith in the Divine is needed by everyone, not only by those facing the threat of death.

We need faith in our day-to-day lives. We need to use the language of faith even when all around us is normal. David exemplified this in the first portion of Psalm 23. "The Lord is my shepherd; I shall want nothing" (Ps. 23:1, NEB), he begins. David recognized God's sovereignty and graciousness during times of normalcy.

You and I should do the same. Even today we should make continual confession of God's abundance to us, giving Him the glory for it. Herein lies a key in the language of faith: it allows God's glory to burn brightly.

The first portion of David's psalm is relevant to three different spheres: the physical, the spiritual and the social.

The Physical Sphere

In the realm of his physical life David declared of God, "He makes me lie down in green pastures" (Ps. 23:2, NEB). When sheep lie down in green pastures it indicates that they have everything they need, that they are satisfied. We are the sheep of our heavenly Shepherd-Father. He lets us lie down in green pastures of restoration. Here David uses the language of faith to paint a picture of peace, an expression of God's goodness. Daily, you and I should make that same declaration.

Many people are prone to make negative declarations. They speak continually of how bad their business is, of how the economic situation is growing worse and worse. Those negative declarations, however, will not help them. By their negative declarations they bring a destructive power into their lives.

Instead of making negative declarations we must be determined to give affirmative confirmations—confessions of creation, victory, and abundance. Envision yourself resting in the green pastures of your business or job, and watch how satisfied you will become. Feed this language of faith into your soul, visualizing God's daily provisions. Then, like David, sing out that you are satisfied every day in the green pastures of your life.

The Spiritual Sphere

David next victoriously stated that God "leads me beside the waters of peace" (Ps. 23:2, NEB). When reading this scriptural statement you can sense spiritual bliss, satisfaction, and peace in your heart. This phrase typifies the blessed fullness of the Holy Spirit, a fullness accurately symbolized by the picture of "waters of peace."

When you confess your sins to God you are cleansed by the blood of Jesus Christ. Then the fountain of life, the precious Holy Spirit, moves into your heart and makes His dwelling there. If you continue to pray and seek God to be filled with the Holy Spirit, Christ will baptize you in the Holy Spirit and fill your heart to overflowing.

If the language of faith is to be potent in your life you must let this verse become a reality. Spiritually, allow our Jehovah God to lead you beside the waters of peace, of fullness in the Holy Spirit. Then the thirst of your soul will be satisfied. You will receive power to serve God with mighty miracles and assurance, your ministry and service unto the Lord becoming richer and more fruitful.

The Social Sphere

When David affirmed, "He renews life within me, and for his name's sake guides me in the right path" (Ps. 23:3, NEB), he was directing the language of faith at his social life.

Amid the daily hubbub of life in our modern society our hearts are often vexed, and our souls feel withered. Sometimes we almost feel it is not worth the effort to wade through the torrential flood of wrongdoing, so strong is its influence.

It is at this juncture that the language of faith gives us the key to victory. We can say aloud with David, "He renews life within me, guiding me in the right path." As we affirm these words repeatedly we feel a strength and comfort rising up within us.

We often do feel powerless when we meet the challenge of a sinful world. Adverse circumstances and the trials of this life try to bind us. We begin to feel weak in our own flesh.

While we cannot live a victorious life by our own determination or by our own strength, the Bible states that God renews life within us. He helps us and guides us in the right path for His name's sake. Declare and affirm that! Speak the language of faith in your social circumstances. When you are lost in the swamp of sinfulness and wrongdoing, speak loudly that God guides you in the right path for His name's sake. Say it over again and again, letting His Word go forth to fight for your victory. Use the language of faith to win your battles in the social sphere.

During Times of Danger

Our lives are not limited to periods of normalcy. We also have times of danger. Danger results for many reasons: sin, weakness, temptation, a fear of death. But even during times of danger David exemplified the importance of the language of faith.

Affirm God's Presence

Let us consider David's language at his time of danger: "Even though I walk through a valley dark as death I fear no evil, for thou art with me" (Ps. 23:4, NEB). David proclaimed that he was not afraid of danger because God was with him. Instead of looking and talking about the "valley dark as death," David affirmed and talked about the presence of God.

When we pass through a valley dark as death we may neither see nor feel the presence of God. But we do not have to. David created the presence of God with his language of faith. He affirmed, "The Lord is with me." David did not see any sign of the Lord's presence, nor did he hear the still, small voice of the Lord. Yet even in that situation he refused to accept the onslaught of circumstantial threats of the dangers in the valley dark as death. He simply affirmed God's presence.

You and I can do the same during our times of danger. When you walk through a valley dark as death do not look at the situation and circumstances around you. They are misleading. If you listen to the language of fear that danger speaks, or are swayed by your feelings, you will be defeated.

Instead, speak the victorious language of faith. By your words affirm the presence of Jesus Christ in the valley dark as death. Declare that Christ is with you in spite of all surrounding danger. Through the spoken language of faith you will feel the presence of Jesus Christ.

Acknowledge God's Protection

David acknowledged God's protection with his words, "Thy staff . . . are my comfort" (Ps. 23:4b, NEB). The shepherd in David's time used the staff to hit any animals that would threaten the safety of the flock. When wild animals tried to attack the sheep the shepherd used his strong and powerful staff to chase them away.

David used this analogy in his language of faith. He compared God to a shepherd, in effect saying, "God carries a staff to protect me." Instead of allowing an awareness of the danger around him to develop, he talked of the God who surrounded and kept him, giving him comfort. David was kept safe through life's wars and conflicts by having learned the language of faith, a language that claimed God's protection.

Declare God's Guidance

In the midst of danger David declared God's guidance: "Thy crook are my comfort" (Ps. 23:4b, NEB). The crook is a long implement curved like a hook on the end. The shepherd would carry his crook with him at all times. When a sheep would begin to wander, the shepherd would stretch out that crook, hook it around the neck of the sheep, and gently pull it back in the right direction. In the same way, God, by the power of the Holy Spirit, leads us in the right way. With danger nearby David learned the language of faith that declared God's guidance.

When everything seems dark without hope, and you feel lost, meandering on the road of life, do not be confused or worried. Instead, use David's language of faith: "I do not know the way, but God is guiding me. Even now, His tender hand is upon my head." As you declare God's guidance you will feel the leading power of God a reality in your life.

In Proverbs we are instructed to: "Put all your trust in the Lord and do not rely on your own understanding. Think of him in all your ways, and he will smooth your path" (Prov. 3:5-6, NEB).

If you and I will declare God's guidance, He will smooth our paths. As David used the language of faith during times of danger, so should we. You and I need not fear danger nor evil, for the Almighty God will be ever with us.

In the Sight of Enemies

In our lives we not only have the dangers caused by evil, but we also have many enemies: doubt, frustration, failure, inadequacy, people bent on our destruction. While in their presence the language of faith continues to be important.

Proclaim God's Provisions

David proclaimed God's provisions: "Thou spreadest a table for me in the sight of my enemies" (Ps. 23:5, NEB). The Lord prepared a table with delicious food within sight of David's enemies. God provided all David needed for strength to carry on, and David proclaimed God's provisions loudly.

Our enemies want us to starve, and to be destroyed. But God's purpose is different. The Lord prepares a table full of provisions, especially for us, in the sight of our enemies. While we proclaim God's provisions with our language of faith, God shows our enemies how gracious He is to His children.

Acknowledge God's Honoring

David acknowledged: "Thou hast richly bathed my head with oil" (Ps. 23:5, NEB). If you pour oil on someone's head on a hot day you refresh that person. To anoint one's head with oil was also a symbol of honor, uplifting one above the others.

The Bible records that God anointed Jesus Christ, and made Him superior to the angels. In the sight of his enemies David acknowledged God's honoring him, virtually saying: "God bathes my head with oil, uplifting me, making me superior to my enemies." God's presence and provisions do the same for us. He makes us superior to our enemies, and we must acknowledge this with our language of faith.

Declare God's Blessings

David further declared, "My cup runs over" (Ps. 23:5, NEB). In the sight of David's enemies God blessed him past his needs. God blessed him with so much that his cup of need ran to overflowing. In the sight of your enemies God will bless you, too, and cause your cup to run over.

In Genesis God made a wonderful promise to Abraham: "I will cause you to become the father of a great nation; I will bless you and make your name famous, and you will be a blessing to many others" (Genesis 12:2, TLB). After that promise Abraham had to go through a long process to learn the language of faith. When he did, he declared God's blessings, blessings that remain with us even today.

As a youth David learned the importance of declaring God's blessings. When he went to fight the giant Goliath he knew God had blessed him with divine favor, and declared this with the language of faith. To a mammoth giant of great strength the youth David declared: "You come to me with a sword and a spear, but I come to you in the name of the Lord of the armies of heaven and of Israel—the very God whom you have defied. Today the Lord will conquer you and I will kill you . . . the whole world will know that there is a God in Israel! And Israel will learn that the Lord does not depend on weapons to fulfill his plans—he works without regard to human means! He will give you to us!" (1 Sam. 17:45-47, TLB).

By his language of faith David built circumstances of victory, causing the mighty Goliath to be defeated. David's language of faith set the scene where God could work. David then ran toward Goliah and, using his sling, tumbled the giant with a stone directly to his forehead. In the sight of the enemy troops on the opposite bank David killed Goliath, bringing God's will to fruition.

David knew the language of faith. Perhaps the most eloquent portion of this language was at the conclusion of David's psalm: "Goodness and love unfailing, these will follow me all the days of my life, and I shall dwell in the house of the Lord my whole life long" (Ps. 23:6, NEB). The conclusion of the language of faith is this: God is faithful, God is good, God gives us His blessings abundantly.

Learn the language of faith. Learn it during times of normalcy, during times of danger, and in the sight of your enemies.

Use the language of faith. During times of normalcy use this language in your physical life, your spiritual life and your social life. During times of danger use the language of faith to affirm God's protection, and declare God's guidance. In the sight of your enemies— whoever or whatever they might be—use the language of faith to proclaim God's provisions, acknowledge God's honoring, and declare God's blessing.

Be assured, whatever the situation, however grave the difficulty: God is faithful, good, and desirous of giving you His abundant blessings. Let the language of faith permeate your life. Let it develop your Christian walk, and deepen your life with Christ. Release God's power with the language of faith, and let the miracles of God flow through you.

2

Finding True Happiness

We all want to be happy.

Many think happiness comes through an abundance of material things. They think they will achieve happiness with wealth and comfort.

Recently two of America's richest men died. At his death billionaire Howard Hughes left a legacy of two billion dollars. Yet he spent the last ten years of his life as a recluse. When he died he left no wife or children to mourn for him. Even with all his wealth, his life and death produced great loneliness.

The second man was the billionaire John Paul Getty. He had accumulated from two to four billion dollars in the oil business. But his private life also was unhappy. He had married and divorced five times. His youngest son had died from pneumonia in 1953, and in 1973 his eldest son had died an alcoholic.

If the abundance of material possessions brought

happiness these two billionaires should have had the greatest happiness in the world. But happiness lies on a more solid and lasting foundation than mere material gain. We need solutions to our deep, inner problems. Without them our lives will be empty of permanent, satisfying meaning, and full of restless unhappiness.

The proper foundation for true happiness consists primarily of three components. Happiness is the combination of these components.

Purpose

The right kind of purpose in your life is an important component in the firm foundation for stable happiness. A life without direction is the life of a vagabond. Where there is no true purpose, there can be no true happiness.

Purpose with Permanence

Even on a physical and material level there must be clear-cut objectives to bring about a secure success. Desire for achievement, however, has one ultimate end: death. Having a temporal purpose in life will therefore never bring a permanent sense of satisfaction and happiness to our lives. For this reason life is often considered a phantom, a deception brimming with disillusionment.

Many people are like Columbus. He set a vague destination for himself, in reality unsure where he was bound. He finally found the West Indies, but never realized where he was. He started home, but did not know which direction to take.

Columbus was fortunate, for he was credited with discovering America. But most are not this fortunate. Instead of discovery their destination is a destitution of meaning, a nagging sense of failure.

I have traveled around the world more than ten times, observing the people in each country I have visited. If the accumulation of material possessions brought happiness, then those who live in the developed nations of Europe and in America should have been the happiest. However, the reverse is often true. Those who purpose the direction of their lives toward materialism—the epitome of temporal goals—seem to be the most miserable of all.

Your life purpose ultimately must be grounded in trust in something beyond this life—in the Eternal. Without this, even the most well-planned and honorable purpose lacks permanence.

Augustine once wrote: "Thou hast made us for thyself, and our hearts are restless until they find their rest in thee." Captured in Augustine's words is the universal purpose of man: to have God in his heart, to have the Eternal caringly guide his every step.

Jesus Christ, God in the flesh, came from heaven and lived among men. He died on the cross in order to save you from nagging emptiness and restless purposelessness. He rose from the grave and returned to heaven, to give you purpose grounded in the Eternal.

Purpose with Identity

Christ understood His purpose on earth, proclaiming, "I know where I come from, and where I am going. . . . I am the way; I am the truth and I am life; no one comes to the Father except by me" (John 8:14; 14:6, NEB). His declaration, bold and simple, shows it is through faith in Christ that we can once again be reconciled to the eternal God. To spend a life of happiness on this earth you must have Jesus Christ as your definite goal and purpose for living. Through Christ we know where we came from, where we are going, and why we are living on earth.

But Christ gives us even more than answers that help us establish our purpose in life. With Him we also have identity.

If we have true faith in Christ, "we are God's children; . . . . We are God's heirs, and Christ's fellow-heirs" (Rom. 8:16, NEB). We not only have purpose with permanence, but we also have purpose with identity.

Purpose with Power

Any purpose without the ability to carry it through is useless. Once you become God's child a reservoir of unlimited power is made available to you. All you need to do is learn how to properly tap into that power reservoir. As one man wrote: "If God is on our side, who is against us?" (Rom. 8:31). The Christian life is not without challenging problems, but it has unlimited resources at its disposal.

Peace

To build happiness you not only need purpose, but you also need peace of mind. But our lives are full of limitations. We live under the limits of our senses, of time, of space, and of unpredictable futures. These boundaries often bring to us a nagging sense of uneasiness, a gnawing discomfort that teeters on the edge of consciousness.

We do not know what is going to happen tomorrow. Unless it is within the ranges of our hearing and vision, we do not even know what is taking place at this very moment.

You hear a knock on your door in the evening. Looking out the window you see a stranger, six feet tall, anxious and formidable. Instantly you feel a sense of uneasiness. Unable to probe into the stranger's mind, you cannot know his intentions. Your limitations are liabilities, and your immediate destiny is a diluted form of despair. Your mind is troubled, far from the peace needed for happiness.

This disease of uneasiness is crippling to one's peace of mind. And it is not limited to the portions of our lives over which we have no control.

The Bondage of Guilt

All of us have made wrong decisions. We have all sinned.

Some sins are open and obvious, easily seen by any who will bother to look. Other sins are kept secret, the arsenal of blackmailers, festering sores that even acts of charity cannot negate.

Often aware of our wrong decisions, of our mistakes and of our sins, we suffer from guilt. This guilt binds us, sapping our strength—mental, physical and spiritual. This bondage of guilt is like little foxes that spoil the grapes of happiness. Unless we are set free, we can never be truly happy. We can never have genuine peace.

The Murk of Meaninglessness

The disease of uneasiness also spreads when we are unable to understand or experience meaning in our lives. If we lose our friends, if we are fired from our jobs, if we grow old, then we become nervous and uneasy. We become fearful that we are losing meaning in our lives.

The dilemma of the elderly is a ready example. Each year thousands of older people suddenly feel left behind by society. Everything and everyone seems to have gone on without them. Lonely, they feel life to be empty. What is worse, many commit suicide—senseless death caused by people who have lost their sense of meaning.

You and I have a continual need for recognition. We want to love and be loved. In the face of a fear of death, we want to carve meaning in our lives.

Some do arrive at a place of meaning. Yet once this meaning is achieved, there follows a constant fear of possible loss. Meaning embedded in the temporal generates a tension, a germ that again infects one with the disease of uneasiness.

The Enemies Defeated

Until we rid ourselves of the uneasiness caused by our limitations, until we are freed from the bondage of guilt, and until we walk clear of the murk of meaning-lessness, we cannot have peace of mind. We cannot have peace in our hearts. To rid ourselves of these enemies to peace is a difficult task, out of the range of human effort.

The only answer is to trust in Jesus. Christ is all-understanding and all-powerful. Through faith in Christ we can be empowered to win the battle against the enemies of our peace of mind. Christ said, "I have been given all authority in heaven and earth . . . be sure of this—that I am with you always, even to the end of the world" (Matt. 28:18-20, TLB). With His death on the cross Christ made ample provision for the peace we so desperately need for happiness.

You may doubt at times whether Christ will do anything for you. There is a Scripture that gives those who have faith this assurance: "Overwhelming victory is ours through Christ who loved us enough to die for us. For I am convinced that nothing can ever separate us from his love. Death can't, and life can't. The angels won't, and all the powers of hell itself cannot keep God's love away. Our fears for today, our worries about tomorrow, or where we are—high above the sky, or in the deepest ocean—nothing will ever be able to separate us from the love of God demonstrated by our Lord Jesus Christ when he died for us" (Rom. 8:37-39, TLB).

Through His death and resurrection Christ has provided resources to combat the enemies of peace. To natural limitations Christ replies, "*Anything* is possible if you have faith" (Mark 9:23, TLB). To the bondage of guilt we can respond: "Who dares accuse us whom God has chosen for his own? Will God? No! He is the one who has forgiven us and given us right standing with himself" (Rom. 8:33, TLB). To the murk of meaninglessness we can proclaim the clarity of Christ. He is the essence and purpose of true peace, giving full and permanent meaning to our lives.

Love and Compassion

The love of Christ provides a basis for a lasting peace of mind. Yet if we are to establish a proper foundation for happiness, we also must have a flow of love and compassion in our own lives.

In our industrialized society life without love—without the touch of sincere compassion—has caused many problems. The family unit is no longer highly valued. People are uprooted, moving from city to city, moving away from stable relationships. The disintegration of the balance we once had has resulted in a loss of restraint. The modern man and woman are floating, soon to be trapped by deceptive and empty attractions.

People are no longer treated as individuals. They are

appraised according to their abilities and monetary worth. Caught in the machinery of daily living, people feel a loss of identity. Some have become anti-social, rebelling against society, searching for identity through crime and perversion. The cancer of dissatisfaction continues to spread, expressing itself in frequent acts of violence. We are no longer living in a fellowship of "I and you," but one of "I and it."

The Wise Old Man

This confusion of values has blocked people from understanding the importance love and compassion hold in relation to happiness. There is a story that vividly illustrates this point.

There was once a wise old man who lived in a small village. All the people in the village greatly respected this man. Whenever they had a problem they would go to him, and ask for guidance.

In the course of their talks the old sage promised the people of the village he would show them the way to happiness. He then asked them to send him a representative, one whom they thought was the happiest person in the village.

The people soon after gathered for discussion, concluding that the most beautiful person would certainly be the happiest. They unanimously chose a beautiful young lady, and sent her as their representative.

Upon seeing the beautiful woman, the old man turned his back. He uttered not a word; his silence a distinct denial.

The people gathered again, this time deciding that the richest person had to be the happiest. They chose the wealthiest man among them, sending him to the wise man.

Seeing their second selection, the wise man became utterly discouraged. He started walking toward a field, and several followed along behind him. Suddenly he stopped. Beside him was a youngster crying, holding a dying sparrow in his hands. "Why are you crying?" asked the wise sage.

Between sobs and tears the young boy replied: "I was walking through this field. As I was going I saw this sparrow. It was hurt so bad. I tried all I know to do to keep it alive. But still it is dying."

An understanding smile spread over the old man's face. Turning to those following him, the wise sage explained; "This is the way to happiness: to have compassion and love for others."

Water into Wine

Neither wealth nor beauty result in happiness, but love and compassion are vital components in bringing a happy life into full bloom. If you cannot live harmoniously with your fellow man, it is impossible for love and compassion to flow freely from you.

The ability to meet and get along well with others can be traced through a process of development. In the beginning of our lives we interact with parents and teachers. Later we usually marry, forming intimate bonds with our mates. Unless we learn to live at harmony in these important relationships we can never experience a solid and permanent happiness in our lives.

After thirty years of research the medical college at The Johns Hopkins University released an interesting finding. They discovered that a lack of proper emotional life causes headaches, ulcers, heart disease, and even cancer. It was further disclosed that patients with cancer were generally introspective and lonely, and had not enjoyed good relationships with their parents and siblings during early childhood. Those who had never learned to share love and compassion were those who tended to disease, and to poor health.

It was to remedy this lack that Christ performed His first miracle. In Cana He attended a marriage—the relationship with the greatest potential for satisfying depth or for devastating disaster. During the wedding feast a need arose, and Christ turned the water into wine.

By this miracle Christ symbolically showed us He has the power to transform our lives from tasteless water into tasty, profitable wine. By this miracle Christ assured us He could transform our lives of emptiness into lives full of love and compassion, satisfying the needs of those around us.

Christ loves you regardless of your education, your wealth, your place in society, your age, your sex or your nationality. Turn your life over to Christ. Let Him flood you with His love. The love of Christ can restore your personality to wholeness, lift your feelings of acceptance, and bring healing to your body, soul and spirit.

Ask Christ to come and change your life. Ask Him to give you more patience and understanding with your family, friends and neighbors. Ask Him to help you to forgive, and bring healing to relationships in need of transformation. And once you receive the love of Christ, start giving the love of God to others. You will be surprised at the joy this will bring you.

To find true happiness establish a purpose with permanence, identity and power. Through faith in Christ you can be freed from the bondage of guilt and the murk of meaninglessness, and released into the peace of mind needed for genuine happiness. When the final component of love and compassion is instilled into your life and attitudes you will find yourself enriched with one of God's greatest blessings, true and lasting happiness.

3

Becoming Prosperous

I once thought that poverty had great moral value. In Korea ministers used to preach that poverty was a blessing, that the poor were those who reaped the most from life's experiences. However, those same ministers were also continually asking their congregations to give more and more money to the church. Teaching the value of poverty, they also preached the merit of increased contributions.

This contradiction bothered me. When I became a minister myself I volunteered to pastor in a slum area of the city of Seoul. People in that community lived lives of poverty, most eating only one meal a day. Children were sick from malnutrition, and many were starving to death. I realized that poverty was not a blessing from God. It was then that I read the Bible anew, searching for a solution. I wanted to know God's will about poverty.

I discovered that God's teaching about poverty was completely different from what was earlier taught in the traditional Korean church. God had never created poverty. When God had created heaven and earth He had created everything in abundance. The Garden of Eden had no deprivation; it was a place of extreme beauty and abundance.

Then Adam and Eve sinned. With sin came judgment. Adam and Eve were forced out of the garden of abundance. The snake—Satan's instrument of temptation—was cursed to crawl on its belly. Eve's curse was pain in childbirth. The land was cursed and Adam, with all men after him, were to "sweat to master it" until death. (Gen. 3:19, TLB). Poverty came as a result of sin.

When Christ came into the world He not only took away our sins, but also came to relieve us from the curses of judgment. "But Christ has bought us out from under the doom of that impossible system by taking the curse for our wrongdoing upon himself" (Gal. 3:13, TLB). Because Christ took away our sins on the cross we no longer need to be under bondage. We can be forgiven, freed from the curse of sin.

There are those who make the fact of Christ's earthly poverty a justification for their own. In many ways Christ was poor, although traveling with Him were a group of women to attend to His material needs and those of His disciples. The Bible states that Christ was poor so that we would not have to be: "You know how full of love and kindness our Lord Jesus was:

though he was so very rich, yet to help you he became so very poor, so that by being poor he could make you rich" (2 Cor. 8:9, TLB). Christ desires that His children of faith be prosperous; however, many are not. They have failed to claim God's blessing of prosperity.

There was a time when many British men went to America to increase their wealth. During this time one poor, young Englishman decided that he also wanted to journey to America to seek his fortune. He conscientiously saved his money, finally with enough to buy a third-class ticket on a boat bound for America. Although he did not have money remaining for food, he decided that his venture was worth the sacrifice.

After he boarded the boat he went down to the third-class section. During mealtime in the dining room he remained alone in the large cabin, pondering the moment when he would arrive at New York's shore.

But that moment was delayed by two weeks. An unexpected typhoon sent the boat off course, and it took fourteen days for the crew to adjust to the originally planned cruise. By the end of those two weeks the young man felt as if he were dying from starvation. Even though he could see New York on the horizon he thought, "Whether I die from starvation, or die from punishment when the restaurant finds that I have no money to pay, it's all the same to me."

So he went to the dining room for the first time, and ordered a full course meal. He devoured the food like a starving man, ordered more, and ate until he was satisfied. Then he turned to the waiter, "Please bring my bill. I need to see the check."

The waiter just looked at him. "What kind of bill do you want, sir?"

"Well," replied the satisfied young man, "I need the bill for all the food I just ate."

"Sir," responded the waiter, "When you bought the ticket to travel on this boat you also purchased all the meals you would need during the trip. You have already paid the bill."

The young man had almost died from starvation. Yet he had already paid for all the food he could have wanted.

Many Christians are like that young man. They receive a ticket to heaven through faith in Jesus Christ. They think they can barely make it to spiritual salvation by believing on Christ. But in that ticket there is also a promise of abundance. Blinded by their own preconceptions they live lives of sparsity, prosperity seeming an impossible feat. If you want to become prosperous, first realize that Christ has already laid the groundwork.

Motivation

In themselves alone, desires for money, fame and prestige never touch the heart of God. God does not give lasting blessings to those who have only selfish aspirations.

When I began my ministry I had wrong motives. As a result I passed through many difficult periods.

Through this I realized the importance of proper motivation in everything the Christian does or desires to do.

If you want to be prosperous, search your heart to find your true motives. Do you want to be prosperous as an avenue to bear more fruit—to be more productive—for God? Do you truly care for others' spiritual welfare, and want to use your prosperity as a channel to bring more people into God's Kingdom?

Place God First

Desire for money alone has even permeated into the ranks of ministers. Several famous evangelists have come to Korea. I remember one of them in particular.

This evangelist came to us several years ago, to conduct a week-long meeting in our church at my request. Before his arrival I launched an extensive advertising campaign, alerting as many as possible to the upcoming revival. For the first two nights the evangelist spoke above-average sermons to large crowds, and many miracles took place.

But before the third night's service he firmly asserted, "I am going to pack and leave immediately."

"What?" I responded in astonishment. "These meetings have been highly advertised. You can't leave. What about the thousands coming every night just to hear you speak?"

"Well," he replied, "there is one way I could stay. If you would give me one thousand dollars more right away, I will stay. If not, I will have to go back to America to raise that amount."

In my heart I burned with anger; ministers were called to preach the gospel, not make money. However, I also knew people would come expecting to hear him. I looked him directly in the eye: "If money is that important to you I'll write you a check right now for $1000. And when you receive that check I am expecting you to preach the remainder of the week."

From that evening on the special presence of the Holy Spirit was absent. No longer did the evangelist's sermons have elements of God's anointing. No longer were the needs of the people touched by God. It was one of the worst revivals our church has ever had. In his sole desire for money that evangelist had lost any spiritual prosperity those remaining meetings could have brought; he also had discouraged us from giving him a previously planned large honorarium.

Our heavenly Father knows our needs, and He will supply them. Our motives and priorities, however, must be properly ordered: "God cares so wonderfully for flowers that are here today and gone tomorrow, won't he more surely care for you, O men of little faith? So don't worry at all about having enough food and clothing . . . your heavenly Father already knows perfectly well that you need them, and he will give them to you if you give him first place in your life and live as he wants you to" (Matt. 6:30-33, TLB).

If you want to become properous it is important for you to have the proper motivation. Place God first in your life, and place your primary desires on the building up of His Kingdom.

Understand Man's Purpose

"Surely you know that you are God's temple, where the Spirit of God dwells. Anyone who destroys God's temple will himself be destroyed by God, because the temple of God is holy, and that temple you are" (1 Cor. 3:16-17, NEB).

God calls us His temple, His home. And the temple of God must have the Spirit of God dwelling within to be of any value. A temple without the Spirit of God is like an empty building, often used to store useless things.

However, if we understand that man's purpose is to be God's temple—God's home—then our perspective becomes sharpened. Then we can more clearly understand why we should be motivated to put God first in our desire to be prosperous. Then we can realize that the Holy Spirit who dwells in us can direct our paths into greater prosperity.

There was one businessman who strongly believed in the guidance of the Holy Spirit. Before every major decision he would close himself in his private office and pray. These prayers for guidance would extend from ten minutes to ten hours.

Even when pressured by associates desperate for immediate response, this businessman refused to settle on a decision. He insisted he must first receive guidance from the Holy Spirit. Every major decision he made—whether he were to buy stocks in a specific firm, merge two companies together, or sell a portion of his business—was based on the Holy Spirit's direction.

It is said he never made one mistake in his major business dealings. Not only did he become one of the wealthiest men in his realm of business, but his advice was the most sought after. And all because he realized the importance of the Holy Spirit's indwelling and the crucial necessity of the Holy Spirit's guidance.

Tithing

Chedorlaomer was King of Elam, an ancient country north of the Persian Gulf. For twelve years Chedorlaomer had been leader of a coalition. This coalition had included the cities of Sodom and Gomorrah, cities of the plain once believed to be situated at the tip of the Dead Sea.

After twelve years many of Chedorlaomer's vassals, involving citizens of Sodom and Gomorrah, rebelled. Genesis records a swift battle between Chedorlaomer and his allies against the rebellious vassals. Chedorlaomer won, the agressive king confiscating everything that was movable—people, animals, food supplies, and valuables. Among the captives was Lot, a nephew of Abram and a citizen of Sodom.

When Abram heard that his nephew had been taken captive he immediately armed his more than 300 trained servants. They pursued the aggressors and overcame them in a remarkable victory. Everything was recovered and every person was retrieved unharmed.

Abram returned with this victory fresh in his memory. Then Melchizedek, king of Salem—thought to be the ancient site of Jerusalem—brought Abram bread and wine. Melchizedek was the priest of the most high God, and he blessed Abram, " 'The blessing of the supreme God, Creator of heaven and earth, be upon you, Abram; and blessed be God, who has delivered your enemies over to you' " (Gen. 14:19-20, TLB).

After receiving this blessing Abram gave Melchizedek a tithe—a tenth of all the spoils Abram had taken. Later God spoke to Abram in a vision: " 'Don't be fearful, Abram, for I will defend you. And I will give you great blessings' " (Gen. 15:1, TLB). God gave Abram promises of prosperity and protection.

The Universal Law of Giving and Receiving

In this account Melchizedek stood as a type of Christ, and Abram represented us Christians. As I looked into the Bible I discovered there are many blessings in tithing, relating to the universal law of giving and receiving.

In the natural world the principle of giving and receiving is prevalent. If a certain type of animal only received life, and refused to give, his species would soon be extinct.

In the Middle East both the Sea of Galilee and the Dead Sea receive their water from the mountains of Lebanon. The Sea of Galilee is full of animals and life, for the water in it is fresh, constantly flowing forth to the Jordan River. The Sea of Galilee both receives and gives, allowing it to be a source of abundance.

The Dead Sea, however, is true to its name. While the Dead Sea receives water from the mountain streams, it has no outlet for giving forth water. The water that flows into it slowly evaporates, leaving salt and other minerals to collect and solidify. Few living things can abide in its waters. Even in the natural realm there must be both receiving and giving. Anything that refuses to give will become useless and dead.

The faithful patriarchs of Israel show us that tithing, an important form of giving to God, is in reality a source of tremendous prosperity. Abram tithed. Isaac and Jacob tithed. In looking at the lives of these men we see they never suffered the effects of poverty for any long periods of time. They were rich men. They all suffered various trials and tribulations, but none died from starvation, and they always had enough to give to others.

In Genesis there is record of a vow Jacob made to God before leaving his home to live with his uncle: " 'If God will help and protect me on this journey and give me food and clothes, and will bring me back safely to my father, then I will choose Jehovah as my God . . . I

will give you back a tenth of everything you give me!"
(Gen. 28:20-22, TLB). Jacob knew the universal law of
receiving and giving. He knew that if he tithed God
would bless him with prosperity.

God later made tithing a commandment: " 'Bring all
the tithes into the storehouse so that there will be food
enough in my Temple; if you do, I will open up the
windows of heaven for you and pour out a blessing so
great you won't have room enough to take it in!' " (Mal.
3:10, TLB). Tithing offers many benefits in our lives,
especially the provisions of protection and prosperity.
If you give to God, He will give even more bountifully
back to you.

How to Tithe

Tithing is meant to be a priority practice, with the
tithe taken from your entire income. "Honor the Lord
by giving him the first part of all your income, and he
will fill your barns with wheat and barley and overflow
your wine vats with the finest wines" (Prov. 3:9-10,
TLB). Tithing—giving one tenth of your income—
carries promises of blessing and prosperity.

When many Christians receive their salaries they
first pay all their living expenses. Then they tithe from
the remaining money. This, however, is not genuine
tithing. Tithing is to be the first fruits of one's entire
income, given to the glory of God. God respects the
faithful who tithe in such a way, and abundantly blesses
them.

Others feel they are the ones to decide the recipient of their tithes. They send their tithes to some small church in the countryside, or to a needy family. This, too, is not genuine tithing. Tithe money should be given to the Lord by giving to the local church where one attends. Remember that Abram paid his tithe to the rich king of Salem. And it was through that king's mouth that Abram received God's blessings.

Whenever you receive the bread and wine of the Word of God, remember to consistently pay your tithes from all your income to your local church. If you do not follow God's pattern in tithing, your tithes will not be recognized. You will be unable to receive the full blessing of prosperity that God desires to give you.

A Practice For Today

Many people argue against tithing. They claim that the practice of paying tithes belonged only to the Old Testament law. However, since we are now living under grace, tithing no longer applies, they reason.

But the practice of tithing is as much alive today as it was during the Old Testament days. Jesus himself stressed tithing. In admonition to hypocritical religious leaders Jesus stated: " 'You tithe down to the last mint leaf in your garden, but ignore the important things—justice and mercy and faith. Yes, you should tithe, but you shouldn't leave the more important things un-done' " (Matt. 23:23, TLB). In this Scripture Christ talked about the importance of tithing, and the need not to lose perspective.

As we look into history and into our own experiences we can see that the practice of tithing has brought many benefits. Throughout history it has been the giving nations that have prospered. This is evident in several Western civilizations, particularly in America. After receiving Christ into their culture and learning from His Word, Americans began to send missionaries, and began to give tithes and offerings to help others. For this reason God has blessed Americans, enabling them to prosper.

The case has been different with the countries of the Orient and Africa. In these areas are vast natural resources. But most countries in these areas have not had the privilege of developing and using those resources. They have denied the gospel of Jesus Christ, and their people have failed to share their material blessings with others.

In Korea there was one man who lived in poverty throughout his youth. At the age of fifty he attended his first church service, listening attentively to a sermon on tithing and the prosperity that would follow. He then felt he should begin to tithe. "Since my income is so small anyway," he thought, "giving a tenth of it to God is going to make little difference."

He later became a Christian, and began to tithe regularly. He had previously never held a steady job. After he began tithing, however, he received a job as a salesman for a steel company. Suddenly he was quite successful, becoming owner of the branch where he worked. After twelve years he became a wealthy man. Even in difficult times this man refused to be discouraged, believing that faithful tithing would lead to prosperity. This man did continue to prosper, all because he had learned the secret of prosperity—tithing.

In another situation there were two men—one a Christian and the other an unbeliever—who decided to establish a business together. The non-Christian partner made twenty thousand dollars a year. The Christian partner, although he made only twelve thousand a year, faithfully tithed each month. However, a strange difference was soon apparent. Even though the non-Christian made more money, he was not prosperous. His family was frequently sick; the medical bills continued to mount, and he carried the load of heavy financial pressure. The Christian man who paid his tithes had prosperity in abundance. Blessed not only in his business, he also had the prosperity of peace and harmony in his personal life.

If you want to become prosperous, do not neglect to pay your tithes to God. Tithing is God's promise of prosperity to His people. And this prosperity is not limited to the material realm. God will also bless you with the prosperity of joy, peace, health, and harmony in your home.

Through Christ's death on the cross the groundwork has been laid for every believer to become prosperous. Our tickets to heaven are not limited to just spiritual salvation, but they also include promises of blessings and prosperity, to be claimed by those with God's faith.

Becoming prosperous is partially a matter of motivation. You and I should understand that man's purpose is to be the temple of God's Holy Spirit, and to desire continually to have the Spirit's direction in our lives. We should put God first in all we do, striving first to further establish God's Kingdom.

Regular tithing to one's local church is a key secret to becoming prosperous, a part of the universal law of giving and receiving. Though instituted in the Old Testament period, tithing is a practice you and I are to continue today, a practice that brings blessing and prosperity. "Now glory be to God who by his mighty power at work within us is able to do far more than we would ever dare to ask or even dream of—infinitely beyond our highest prayers, desires, thoughts, or hopes" (Eph. 3:20, TLB).

4

Improving Your Self-Image

Central to genuine success is a positive and realistic self-image. But throughout the course of any given day we are exposed to negative feedback. Throughout the course of our lives we frequently harbor damaged self-images. We want to break free, to discover our full potentials, but we cannot. Greater than our desire for expansion is the need to be consistent with our poor self-images. Unsatisfied with who we are, we try to imitate others.

When I began my ministry I had little success with many of my sermons. My self-image as a preacher was low, and my frustration was mounting.

I first wanted to be like Billy Graham. I often listened to his sermons, and even memorized a few. When I spoke at my church I tried to preach like he did. I would start off my sermons: "Ladies and gentlemen!" But by the time I reached the middle of a sermon I would be

breathing very hard, and would be completely exhausted. I realized I could not be like Billy Graham.

I next decided I wanted to be like Oral Roberts. I
tried to preach in Oral Roberts's own dynamic style,
waiting for similar results to occur in my congregation.
But nothing happened. I felt completely discouraged.
"God," I prayed, "I want to be like Billy Graham or like
Oral Roberts. Please help me!"

Then the Holy Spirit spoke to my heart: *"My son, I
need only one Billy Graham and one Oral Roberts in
this world. I want you to be the one and only PAUL
YONGGI CHO."*

Hindrances to a Positive Self-Image

It is the same with us all. God made each of us to be
unique creatures, each with an individual self-image. It
is our responsibility to build our self-images, to explore
and expand our God-given potentials. There are, however, hindrances we need to be aware of if we are to
develop fully.

One hindrance involves the continual habit of self-
depreciation. Many people put themselves down, pointing to their inabilities. They might have an intense
desire to enter a specific field, but their constant under-
estimation of their capabilities continually discourages
them from doing so. They live their lives in mediocrity,
never becoming what they might have been.

Others are hindered by a false sense of security.
Though they may be dissatisfied with themselves, they

fear the danger of risk even more. In the privacy of their minds they reason: "I have a nice job, a nice business. Even though I sometimes think I could be more, I'd better play it safe. I'd better settle down in what I am now, and be content."

Competition is a hindrance to some. Their greatest fear is failure; their greatest enemy, themselves. They live out their lives quietly, never comprehending the adventure of living.

For most the greatest enemy to a healthy self-image is a memory sharp with the details of past failures, guilt and condemnation. Sometimes these people will even deny themselves the healing of their memories, more comfortable with the accusations of the past than the aspirations of the future.

But no matter what is hindering your development of a positive self-image, you can overcome it by implementing the following five steps.

Utilize Your Imagination

Many suffer because of a negative way of thinking. They feel their physical condition is hopeless, that they are a failure in their business, or that no one loves them. God works through man's imagination. As long as one allows these negative thoughts to be dominant, God himself is blocked from helping that person, for imagination is even stronger than will power in controlling a person.

There was a former alcoholic who had not had a

drink for six years. One hot summer day he began to daydream; he thought how good a beer would taste. "Besides, only one would be quite harmless," he thought.

He then went to a bar, and drank a bottle of beer. Since that time he has resumed his old habit. If he had not allowed his imagination to indulge in that daydreaming he would have been saved from the self-image of an alcoholic.

I knew an obese woman who had been to several doctors and hospitals. She tried various kinds of medicines, and many types of methods. These would help her a little, but the results would never be lasting. She eventually became deeply depressed, eating constantly.

Then she decided to change her self-image by using her imagination. She began to visualize herself as being slender. Her appetite for food soon began to decrease. She lost weight, and is now thin.

The Bible teaches us about the importance of using our imaginations. The story of Adam and Eve is one example. Eve was tempted by Satan to eat fruit from the forbidden tree. Allowing the words of Satan to simmer in her mind, they filled her imagination. Eve continued to look at the fruit, and to think how good it would be. She then developed a tremendous desire to eat the forbidden fruit. In spite of her strong will power she was drawn to that fruit, and ate it. She then gave some to her husband Adam.

Through this act, visualized in Eve's imagination,

both Adam and Eve fell. Through their sin they developed the self-image of fallen man. It was only through the sinless life, death and resurrection of Christ—the second Adam—that full provision was made for man to be restored to a healthy self-image.

If you want to change your self-image, start by changing your imagination. I suggest that you let your imagination dwell on the threefold blessing of God mentioned in this verse: "Beloved, I pray that in all respects you may prosper and be in good health, just as your soul prospers" (3 John 2, NAS). Here God lists a threefold blessing that He desires you to have. God wants you to be prosperous in the spiritual realm, in the physical realm, and in the material realm.

With this Scripture as a basis, imagine yourself growing in your spiritual life. Imagine your business becoming prosperous. Imagine your body being touched by the healing power of God. Visualize yourself under this threefold blessing, showered upon you by God's power. Let your mind dwell on these things, and God will begin to create a renewed self-image in you.

Establish a New Identity

If you identify yourself with a low self-image, you will continue to view yourself poorly. Not only must you use your imagination to change your self-concept, you must also utilize your mind and efforts to establish a new identity—an identity free of self-depreciation, free of a false sense of security, free of the memory and

47

fear of failure, free of guilt and condemnation.

It might seem impossible to locate the focal point of such an identity. But with Christ all things are possible. By putting our faith in the heavenly Father and in Jesus Christ we can become creative and victorious people with new identities. I know this through my own experience.

I was born in Korea during the Japanese Occupation. Our conquerors of this period prided themselves on their origins, and continually degraded our Korean heritage. Even in our own land we were considered third-rate citizens. Our entire population suffered from a low national self-concept.

When I was a high school student my country was invaded by the communists, an invasion that was to mark the beginning of the Korean War. The war took what little we had away, and my family lived in dire poverty. There were days when the next meal proved a primary uncertainty, and nights when disease filled my body with pain.

But when I accepted Jesus Christ as my personal Savior I immediately knew I was different. I was a child of the King of kings and Lord of lords. I talked to God as if He were my own friend. I changed and began to develop a tremendous positive attitude toward my own thoughts, my own life, and my own self-image. Through faith in Jesus Christ I rose above the physical, mental, and spiritual poverty of my situation. I had a new identity.

I discovered that becoming a Christian meant that I received a new nationality. You may be a citizen of England, France, Germany, or America; I am a citizen of Korea. But when we put our faith in Christ, each of us becomes a citizen of the Kingdom of Heaven. "For He has rescued us out of the darkness and gloom of Satan's kingdom and brought us into the kingdom of his dear Son" (Col. 1:13, TLB).

My new identity in Christ also meant I had a new position. Most think we Christians are just common people, simply looking for something better. But when we became Christians we ceased being common. By the grace of Jesus Christ you and I are seated in heavenly places. Even though we physically live in our individual countries, spiritually we are seated with Christ on the right hand of the Father. "God . . . lifted us up from the grave into glory along with Christ, where we sit with him in the heavenly realms—all because of what Christ Jesus did" (Eph. 2:6, TLB).

With my new identity I also have found I had a new kind of life. When we were born as humans we received a human nature. We now are destined to enjoy God's kind of life eternally. This is the difference between the believer and the unbeliever: the unbeliever only has natural life. The believer also has God's life.

If you base your new identity on the temporal you will be disillusioned. Christ offers you much more: a new nationality that will give you pride and confidence; a new position of security and opportunity for creative adventure; a new life with sins forgiven, and guilt and condemnation erased. Come to Christ, and establish a new identity you can develop into eternity.

Set Definite Goals

Man is a goal-seeking organism. His personality is controlled not as much by his past accomplishments and present environment as by his future goals.

I have counseled tens of thousands of people, most of whom are facing failure. They had no definite goals in their lives and had accomplished little of substance. An unfocused life is a wasted life, and a wasted life is most open to a low self-image. If you have no goal, where will you focus your abilities? How will you direct your life? But if you set a definite God-directed goal you will be successful. That success may be big or it may be small, but it will still be success.

You must have definite goals in your daily living. Every morning write down the goal you want to accomplish for that particular day. Write a yearly goal. Let your life become totally concentrated and focused on these goals. Let your heart's neon sign flash your goals brightly and constantly in your mind. Then, as you seek after God according to your goals, your self-image will be influenced and improved, your achievements will become building blocks for a higher self-concept.

Scientists say that a man uses only 10 percent of his abilities throughout his lifetime. So, during your life you also need a definite, ultimate and eternal goal. This eternal goal is eternal life in heaven through faith in Jesus Christ, and life on earth for the glory of God. This should be your ultimate and eternal goal. Even though you become successful in everything you do—business, politics, school, society and family—if you do not have this ultimate, eternal goal, you will never have the satisfaction necessary for a healthy self-image.

Speak Positive Words

Many use their daily language promiscuously. This is very dangerous. The spoken word is the basic material with which God created the universe. God has given us the ability to speak and express ourselves with words. By the spoken word we create our universe of circumstances.

Most think we live our lives by outward appearances, but that isn't true. Through the spoken word you create either an image of success or an image of failure.

Let me illustrate the power of the spoken word. I might say, "It is very cold today. It is so cold that the water pipes are frozen, and there are icicles on the roof."

You immediately form a picture of a cold, wintry day. You can almost hear the cold wind blowing. You can almost see the snow falling around you. That picture might become so vivid in your mind that you wonder where you left your winter jacket, or how you might find your fall sweater.

Then let me say, "It is extremely hot today. It is so hot that I can hardly stand to have clothes on my body."

Your image of the day changes, and you can almost feel the hot sun, the air in the room warm and stuffy. Your breathing will grow more shallow, and your thirst for a cool drink will increase.

I have talked about the same day. But my words have been different, as have your images of that day.

Christ understood the power of the spoken word. When Jesus met Simon He changed his name to Peter. In Hebrew "Simon" meant "reed," and indicated a personality swayed by blowing winds, altered by shifting opinions. But "Peter" meant rock. It portrayed a picture of someone stable, unbendable, and dependable. So every time someone called Peter's name, a positive affirmation of a changed self-concept was drilled into his mind. He was no longer the bendable reed, but the dependable rock. And each time he said his own name, he affirmed a positive self-image. Peter, Peter, Peter; rock, rock, rock. It is not surprising that Peter developed into one of the more stable and dependable of all Christ's apostles.

We all occasionally have disappointments. But we should never allow disappointments to trigger negative words of resentment and anger, words that lead to self-pity and depression, words that lead to clouded self-concepts.

Improve your self-image with positive spoken words. God promised us "that all that happens to us is working for our good if we love God and are fitting into his plans" (Rom. 8:28, TLB). Knowing God's promise, you can speak positively. You can be in an attitude of praise to God, even in the most difficult situation. So guard your words and guide your self-image to heights in the heavenlies.

Exercise Positive Faith

But it is often not enough to speak positive words. You must also exercise positive faith in the self-image you have visualized in your imagination. As a person with a new identity you must expand into a faith life, confident in the definite goals you have set.

Everyone is born with a certain amount of human faith. If geniuses did not have faith in themselves, they could not accomplish great achievements. There is also the case of mediocre students who do not do well in school, but after they graduate, they somehow achieve shining accomplishments. These former students put faith into action, and with confidence in an elevated self-image, exhibit outstanding abilities.

The same is true on a spiritual level. For the best and only real lasting results, human faith should be linked into God. The work of God is faith, for He can create anything in this life. If you put your faith into God's faith, God's faith is going to bring forth God's ability and God's power in you, empowering you to improve and maintain a healthy self-image.

If you want to improve your self-image, begin by utilizing your imagination. Visualize positive thoughts. Establish a new identity based on Christ, and you will discover a new nationality, a new position, and a new kind of life. Never neglect the setting of definite goals, and the importance of speaking positive words. Above all, exercise positive faith. Allow God to improve your self-image, and you will become a shining light to a dark and needy world.

5

Building Right Relationships I

The Right Foundation

A healthy and realistic self-image is important. Your self-image is your relationship with yourself, influencing everything you do. But what about your relationship with others? How can they be properly built?

To an extent, the building of a healthy relationship can be compared to the building of a house. Beginning with the solid ground of a good self-image you then construct a strong foundation. Without this strong foundation any relationship that follows will suffer.

Your Character

A strong foundation has two aspects. One is the provision of an Almighty God. The other is the development of a stable character, a character with the traits of honesty, faithfulness and perseverance.

Honesty

While traveling in Europe I came across many large and elaborate buildings. One in particular remains vivid in my memory. It was a beautiful house, eloquently designed with the most modern furnishings and equipment, lovely to behold.

But no one used the house. Government officials would not even permit anybody to enter the building. While it was under construction, some of the men in charge had been bribed. They had used vastly inferior materials, building the house on a false foundation. Millions of dollars were spent in building that house. But dishonesty had prevailed. Even today that beautiful house cannot be used.

Those who live with falsehoods and dishonesty cannot construct the foundation that is needed to build right relationships. Though they might be attractive to look at, the people who truly know them will avoid close contact. They will lack the comfort of genuine friendship, harming all who dare befriend them.

We must also be honest with God if we want to build a productive spiritual relationship. This truth is graphically portrayed in a passage in Luke. An account in chapter eighteen contrasted the prayer of a proud, self-righteous religious leader to that of a cheating tax collector.

The religious leader prayed: "Thank God, I am not a sinner like everyone else, especially like that tax collector over there! For I never cheat, I don't commit adultery, I go without food twice a week, and I give to God a tenth of everything I earn."

The corrupt tax collector stood apart from the religious leader, not even daring to raise his eyes to heaven. He beat his chest in sorrow, exclaiming, "God, be merciful to me, a sinner" (Luke 18:11-13, TLB).

The religious leader denied his sinfulness. In his dishonesty with God he blocked the establishment of genuine relationship with his heavenly Father. But the tax collector was different. He had done wrong in robbing the people with unfair tax assessments. He was honest about his sin, and confessed it to God. Because of his honesty God's forgiveness could flow. The tax collector had the beginnings of a right relationship with God. Open honesty is needed for all relationships to be properly founded.

Faithfulness

Our world is full of the unfaithful. Husbands are unfaithful to their wives, and wives to their husbands. Never before has divorce—the absolute disruption of the most intimate of human relationships—been so common. Bureaucrats cheat their governments, company workers are unfaithful to their employers, and friends betray friends. Unfaithfulness is a prevalent problem in our modern society, and it is one reason for the poor development of good relationships.

Faithfulness benefits those on both sides of a given relationship. I read a story about a man working in a department store in Pittsburgh, Pennsylvania. It was raining outside, and not many people were shopping.

While the other clerks chatted with each other, one male clerk noticed an old woman who was looking around. Although he could see she was just passing time, the clerk invited the elderly woman to come to his office and rest. He seated her in a comfortable chair, asking if he could be of any help. She told him she was just waiting for a friend to come by and pick her up.

The clerk went outside several times, looking for her friend. He finally found her friend, and brought her to the woman waiting in his office. He did not have to be courteous. But he was a faithful worker, allowing his careful consideration to extend into every encounter.

The elderly woman and her friend left. Several days passed, and the clerk received a beautiful thank-you card. The thank-you card was signed by Andrew Carnegie, owner of the great American Steel Corporation, and son of the elderly lady he had invited to wait in his office.

The clerk's kind act was not soon forgotten. Carnegie later needed to order materials for a development project he was financing in Scotland. Carnegie's mother strongly urged him to order the furniture from the store the faithful clerk worked in. The large orders of furniture from that store increased its worth by millions of dollars. The young clerk became a successful businessman. He had been faithful to his job, exceeding his responsibility. His faithfulness had initiated a relationship that was to benefit him the rest of his life.

Christ illustrated the importance of faithfulness with a story of a man who was traveling to another country. Before he left he called together his servants, giving them money to invest while he was away.

He divided the money according to each servant's abilities, entrusting the equivalent of $5,000 to one, $2,000 to another, and $1,000 to the last. He then left on his journey.

The servant with $5,000 immediately began to buy and sell with it, earning another $5,000. The second servant with $2,000 was also faithful to his master's trust, and earned an additional $2,000. But the last servant simply dug a hole in the ground, and hid the money for safekeeping.

After a period of time their master returned, asking his servants to give an account of his money. The man he had entrusted with $5,000 gave him $10,000 back. "You have been faithful in handling this small amount," the master said, "so now I will give you many more responsibilities. Begin the joyous tasks I have assigned to you."

The second servant reported: "Sir, you gave me $2,000 to use, and I have doubled it."

"Good work," responded his master. "You are a good and faithful servant. You have been faithful over this small amount, so now I will give you much more."

Then the third servant came: "Sir, I knew you were a

hard man, and I was afraid you would rob me of what I earned, so I hid your money in the earth and here it is!"

The master grew angry, realizing that the servant's reasoning was just an excuse for his lack of faithfulness. "Wicked man!" replied the master. "Lazy slave! Since you knew I would demand your profit, you should at least have put my money into the bank so I could have some interest.

"Take the money from this man," he commanded, "and give it to the man with the $10,000. . . . throw the useless servant out" (Matt. 25:21-30, portions from TLB).

The servants who were faithful with their master's trust continued to develop a firm and lasting relationship. The unfaithful servant, however, was rejected, never to be allowed in the fellowship of his master again.

Perseverance

In building solid foundations for relationships it is important for us to be honest, and it is important for us to be faithful. But neither honesty nor faithfulness have full impact unless we also persevere. The Bible teaches the basic principle of perseverance in the verse: "Ask, and you will be given what you ask for. Seek, and you will find. Knock, and the door will be opened" (Matt. 7:7-8, TLB). Asking requires only the use of the voice; seeking requires only a probing look. Knocking, however, requires a more definite action. If we desire something enough we must be consistent and diligent. If we want to build a good relationship we must persevere past obstacles.

In my travels I have visited many countries. While journeying I have noticed a pattern. In countries that lie in warm, southern regions there are natural resources to be found, but the people tend to be idle in the heat, and the countries are consequently termed "underdeveloped." However, in the countries in the North, even where natural resources are more limited, the people have more perseverance. In their diligent efforts they use what is accessible; these countries are often the developed nations.

Perseverance is also needed to develop the resources of a relationship. And the ones who persevere best are the people who have learned to withstand the seasonal changes that life brings.

God's Provisions

An honest and faithful character that possesses perseverance provides important elements needed in the foundation of a healthy relationship. But human character has flaws, and many moments of weakness. It is crucial in our relationships with others that we first have a relationship with the One who never changes, the One who will never fail us. That is why a strong foundation also must be built with elements only God can provide: an eternal relationship and an enduring enjoyment.

An Eternal Relationship

You and I, and all mankind of past and present, have sinned. We have, like Adam and Eve, broken our trust and relationship with God. In Old Testament times God-ordained sacrifices were symbolic acts, temporary restorations of man's relationship to God. Then Christ came to earth. His death on the cross was the ultimate sacrifice; His life was resurrection proof of God's power in man's every situation.

Through faith in Christ we are saved from the final end of sin: a death that brings eternal agony and separation from God. Through a saving faith in Christ our relationship with God is established throughout eternity. Though we still make mistakes, we have God's continual forgiveness. Though we are still weak, Christ gives us His strength. And with an eternal relationship like that our other relationships have a stability never before available to them.

In the Orient the father is an authoritarian figure. When I was a young boy I had a deep fear of my father, a fear developed by Korean society's values and by my father's stern words. I disliked my father, and felt best when I could avoid him.

When I was a young man I turned from my family's religion of Buddhism and became a Christian. As a result of my decision I was thrown out of my home, and ostracized by my family. Though I felt the separation keenly, in my loneliness I knew I needed an eternal relationship with God more than the comfort of family ties.

My love for my family continued, and I believed the Scripture: "Believe on the Lord Jesus and you will be saved, and your entire household" (Acts 16:31, TLB). I put my faith in that Scripture and began to pray three times a day for the salvation of my family.

I wrote letters to my father, but he would not answer. Cast out from my home for about one year, my prayers became more desperate. Yet my father became harder and harder.

I continued praying for two years, and then heard that my father's stocking and glove business had gone bankrupt. He had lost everything. Not long after, he came to Seoul, looking pale and dirty.

He had come to see me: "You are the one causing all my trouble," he accused. "Since you became a Christian nothing has gone right for me. Buddha and the spirits of our ancestors are angry with us. I've failed in my business and there is no way for me to recover. I want to commit suicide right here in front of you. I want to pay you back for all my troubles. Then you must take care of your mother and the other children."

I was attending Bible school at that time, and my father stayed in a nearby area. I continued to pray for my father, and told my friends about him. They offered to go out and help him sell his stockings and gloves. Then I went to my father and said, "If you will attend one chapel service my friends will help you sell your wares."

When my father heard this he was pleased. Though still not favorable toward Christianity, he was concerned about selling his apparel, and agreed to attend the chapel service.

During that chapel service I was to interpret the sermon of an American missionary. When the American missionary began to preach I silently cried out to God to help me use this opportunity to the fullest. While the minister preached one sermon, I preached another, directed entirely at my father.

Suddenly my father lifted his head. He opened his eyes wide, and seemed to be listening intently. Then he bent over and began to cry. However, I was not sure whether his tears were tears of repentance, or the tears of a man who had failed in business.

When the service was over the students filed out, and my father alone remained. I walked down and very carefully lifted him up. "Father," I asked, "what happened to you?"

When he turned to look at me, his face shone as the sun; I knew God had touched his heart. "Father," I exclaimed, "you are a Christian!"

"Son," he responded, "listen to me. In the beginning when I came here, I was criticizing you. I thought I knew better than all those students, and the service was too long.

"But suddenly my eyesight clouded and I couldn't see anything. Jesus appeared and He called my name. He asked me how long I was going to resist Him.

"I saw Jesus. I know He is the living God. I cried out my sins to Him, and now I have peace and confidence. I am happy."

We spent the next moments together in great joy. We had long been alienated, first by my fear of my father's authority, and later by ostracism because of my belief in Christ. But now we both had an eternal relationship with God, and on that basis we became closer and more trusting than had ever before been possible. We walked out of the chapel, hand in hand.

By then it had begun to snow. "Father," I remarked, "it is snowing now. You should be able to sell a lot of stockings, socks and gloves."

"Son," he responded, "I'm not concerned about that now. Look at those pine trees. I've never seen trees so beautiful."

My father's heart had changed, and his whole world became new. Full of joy he said, "Tomorrow I'm going down to the country. I am going to tell your mother about my new relationship with God."

The next day he rode the train, returning to our family. Because my father had returned home without having sold anything they were frightened. Like the rest of the family, my mother thought he was going to be angry. She lay awake all night, in fear of that supposed anger.

Seeing the family's reaction, he was ashamed he had not sold anything, and did not tell anyone he had become a Christian. When the morning church chimes rang, my father kneeled and prayed: "Heavenly Father, forgive me for having hated my wife. For so long I have mistreated her. Now please forgive me. Since you have come into my heart, Jesus, I have a new love for my wife and family. I no longer want to rule them with fear, but tenderness."

My mother heard my father's prayer. She was so moved that she responded: "I want to be a Christian, too." Then they tenderly embraced.

In my whole life, I had never seen my mother and father kiss and hug each other. But when Christ came into their lives, all things became new. My brothers and sisters saw my parent's new tenderness. They sent me a telegram to come quickly, ready to hear my message.

I rode the train back home, returning to the same place from which I had once been cast out. I preached the message of Jesus Christ to my entire family. Since that time all eleven members of my family have been saved.

Established on our eternal relationships with God through faith in Jesus Christ, our entire family grew in love and respect for each other. We have been able to develop deepening relationships that previously had been impossibilities.

An Enduring Enjoyment

Through the sacrifice of His sinless life, Jesus Christ provided a way for us to have an eternal relationship with God. But without the Holy Spirit we will never fully receive all the blessings that an eternal relationship with God through Christ can bring. God has ordained that the Holy Spirit would help us enjoy His blessings. Without the power of the Holy Spirit, we are powerless to enjoy God's riches.

When talking about the coming of the Holy Spirit, Christ said: "When the Holy Spirit, who is truth, comes, he shall guide you into all truth, for he will not be presenting his own ideas, but will be passing on to you what he has heard. . . . he will show you my glory" (John 16:13, 15, TLB). And nothing on earth can be more glorious than the blessings that Christ, through the Holy Spirit, showers on those who have faith.

The Holy Spirit aids us in enjoying God's blessing in three ways: by dwelling with us, by dwelling within us, and by anointing us with God's power. The enduring enjoyment of these blessings is an essential element in further developing our relationship with God, and building a right foundation to our relationships with others.

When we receive Jesus Christ as our personal Savior we also have a relationship with the Holy Spirit. The Holy Spirit dwells with us, like the atmosphere engulfing the entire earth and all human beings. He is the one who adds pressure so that we will open our hearts to receive Jesus Christ. The Holy Spirit is constantly pointing out sin, showing God's provision of eternal life as an alternative.

But the Holy Spirit does not stay like an atmosphere around us. He comes into our spirits and makes our bodies His dwelling temple. And through His indwelling, the Holy Spirit imparts to us knowledge and revelation about Jesus Christ and God's Word, the Bible. As a result, we gain a new dimension of life and knowledge. We learn to live a full life, a life filled with enjoyment of God's rich blessings.

The Holy Spirit also anoints us with power, power to minister God's blessings to others. Christ wants to work His ministry through you and me. But without the anointing of the Holy Spirit, we are not equipped to become the channel through which Christ can flow to meet the needs of others. For this reason we all need the baptism of the Holy Spirit. It is when the Holy Spirit baptizes us that our Christian lives can become even more dynamic and powerful.

Each Christian must therefore develop a relationship with the Holy Spirit. Without this relationship, you and I cannot fully enjoy the many blessings God wants to give us. Without a developing relationship with the Holy Spirit you have just been licking the outside of the watermelon.

Be aware of the Holy Spirit's presence around you. Welcome His presence as He makes you God's dwelling temple. Allow Him to anoint you with power for ministry. Then you will learn to enjoy more of God's blessings. You will have cut the watermelon. You will be enjoying the taste of the sweet pulp inside, tastes of enjoyment that will endure throughout your Christian life.

6

Building Right Relationships II

The Right Building Materials

Once the foundation has been properly laid and given time to settle and set, the building of the house structure can begin. Upon the strong foundation of God's provisions for an eternal relationship and an enduring enjoyment, and upon an honest and faithful character of perseverance, a lasting and beautiful relationship can be built. The construction of a healthy relationship, however, cannot be made with haphazardly chosen values and priorities. The right building materials must be used.

Christ the Cornerstone

Several years ago when the walls of a building were being constructed a cornerstone represented the initial starting place in the construction of a large and important building. The placement of the cornerstone determined the angle of the other walls. If the cornerstone was faulty the entire building would often be in error, with consequent weakness which lessened the building's safety.

In the building of all our relationships there is a cornerstone. For some it is a cornerstone of social convenience. In those relationships one is a friend to another because it seems proper or because there is a certain amount of mutual social benefit. The social-convenience cornerstone, however, is small and weak. That relationship can never develop, nor will it be able to weather the deep troubles life often brings.

Other relationships have the cornerstone of immediate personal need. One person needs something another has, and with that guiding principle a relationship is built. There are even some marriages that are built on a joint cornerstone of immediate personal need. But lust can never take the place of love, money can never replace the wealth of integrity, and improved social acceptance is never an adequate substitute for honesty. The cornerstone of immediate personal need marks a relationship with impending failure.

There are many types and qualities of relationship cornerstones. Some are more stable or more beautiful than others. But no matter how noble a cornerstone may seem, if it is born of human effort and desire alone, it will not last. Those involved will not develop as they could have.

There is, however, a perfect cornerstone. This

cornerstone is flawless; the guidance it promotes builds relationships where further development is always encouraged. This cornerstone is eternal; the relationships built with its direction can withstand storms of sorrow, floods of fear, and hurricanes of helplessness. This cornerstone is Jesus Christ.

Christ lived a life without sin. He is our ultimate example in all we do, especially in the building of our relationships with others. By reading God's Word, the Bible, we can more fully comprehend the values, priorities and principles that Christ taught and exemplified. Through prayer, the Holy Spirit can more clearly show us the directions our lives and relationships need to take. Through fellowship with believers we can catch glimpses of Christ in others, and more fully understand how Christ wants to work through us.

Jesus Christ must not be just your Savior. Jesus Christ must not be just your daily Provider. Jesus Christ must also be the Lord of your relationships, Christ the Cornerstone.

Commitment and Love

During the Korean War one young pregnant woman was fleeing south to freedom. Friendless, she braved the struggle of the winter trip. As she came near the end of her journey she suddenly felt the pains of childbirth approaching.

Needing help, she wanted to reach a nearby town where two American missionaries were living. Even though she hurried as quickly as possible she finally had to stop and deliver her baby under a small bridge. It was bitter cold, and after the baby boy's birth she tried desperately to keep the child warm. She wrapped her body and clothes around the infant, letting her warmth keep him alive.

Early the following morning, as the missionary couple was driving on the small bridge, the American woman thought she heard a baby crying. They stopped their car and the husband went under the bridge to investigate. There the husband found a naked woman, frozen to death, clutching a small bundle.

The baby had almost died from the icy cold winter wind, but because of the warm clothes, he was still barely breathing. After burying the woman on the side of the mountain in a special grave, the couple took the infant boy home with them. During the years that followed they raised him as their own son.

Then it came time for him to enter school. The young child repeatedly asked his missionary parents about his own father and mother. Eventually the missionary couple told him what had happened. It is said that after he discovered his true origins he found his mother's grave. Taking off his clothes, he placed them on that grave, wetting the ground with his tears.

Commitment. It is a word to many and a reality to a few. Without true commitment relationships cannot be properly built, fully developed or long-lasting. Commitment, especially when triggered by love, is one of the finest building materials used in constructing a right relationship. Because of commitment the young infant lived. Because of commitment you can give new life to the lives of the needy around you.

Christ loved and was committed to all who came to Him, despite their doubts and weaknesses. He healed the hurt, encouraged the brokenhearted, fed the hungry, led the self-righteous into truth, and gave solution to the searching. He accepted each person as he was and was committed to meet every need.

Christ was committed in His relationships with His disciples, committed to develop the best in each one. While He was with them He gave them truth and power. With His death He gave us all His very self.

Peter was one of Christ's disciples who was touched by the rich blessings in Christ's commitment. It was Peter who wrote: "Do you want more and more of God's kindness and peace? Then learn to know him better and better. For as you know him better, he will give you, through his great power, everything you need for living a truly good life: he even shares his own glory and his own goodness with us! And by that same mighty power he has given us all the other rich and wonderful blessings he promised" (2 Pet. 1:2-4, TLB).

Christ's example of love and commitment to us shows how we are to be committed to others. We must accept others as they are, and learn to love them. We must be committed to those we develop relationships with, committed to meet their needs and to bring out the best in them. And that commitment must have an element of sacrifice. That commitment must have a measure of love.

Positive Confirmation

As the silkworm builds its cocoon by the threads of its mouth, so you build your relationships with your words. If you criticize and complain, speaking negative thoughts and dreams, your relationships will suffer. In building solid relationships you need to minister positive words of confirmation. You need to build others up, show them their genuine importance, and let them know you are grateful for their friendship.

Once my wife almost left me. Everyday when I arrived home I began to criticize her: "Honey, the house isn't clean. Honey, the towels are dirty in the bathroom."

Then I would wander into the kitchen: "Honey, what are you doing? These dishes aren't washed very well. Look at this spoon. It's not completely clean. What do you do in the house all day, anyway?"

I felt that my criticism was constructive. As head of the house, I felt I was right in my close inspection. But slowly the smile began to disappear from my wife's face. She became increasingly depressed. She wanted to leave me.

I started praying, "Lord, I give her a lot of money. I buy nice clothes for her. I let her live in a nice house, and feed her well. Why should she be depressed? Why can't she be happy?"

Then the Holy Spirit spoke to my heart, "Cho! You are a sinner, so why do you want your wife to be a perfect person? If you constantly measure your wife by your standards of perfection, she will not even be able to stand your presence. Your wife does not need a self-righteous husband. Your wife needs a loving husband. She needs words of positive confirmation if your relationship is to be developed."

Since that time I have responded to my wife differently. When I walk into our home I compliment her on her hard work. I admire how well the table is set for meals, and how much effort she puts into keeping the house in order. I compliment her on how nice she looks and on how much she means to me.

She has responded to my words of positive confirmation. The smile has reappeared on her face. Our relationship has broken free of negative constrictions. We are now sharing the best time we have ever had in our relationship.

Affirmative Action

I also learned that while words of positive confirmation were vital in building a good relationship, they were still not enough. My words had to be followed with affirmative action. I also had to show that by my deeds I appreciated, loved and treasured my wife. When words and action are combined, the results are more complete.

A Jewish man was going down from Jerusalem to Jericho when he was attacked by thieves. The thieves stole everything he had. They took all his clothes, beat him, and left him both naked and near death.

Then a man came toward him. The dying man expected the traveler to help him. As the traveler came nearer, he recognized him as a priest. But the priest, symbol of the law, did not help him.

Law just carries out judgment and death. Law only exposes. If we, like the priest, become as the law to others in relationships, we will avoid helping them. In reality our own pious strictness prevents us, a lesson I had learned in my relationship with my wife.

A second man came by the beaten Jew. We can imagine the needy man started to shout: "Mister, come and help me!"

As the second traveler came near he could be recognized as a Levite. Levites assisted in the temple. This Levite symbolized ritualism, outward forms of empty tradition.

We are often Levites, trying traditional ways of building relationships. Men begrudgingly buy flowers for their wives. Friends flatter friends, then gossip about the other's faults. Bosses commend employees on their good work, still refusing them raises and real recognition. These are the Levites, full of form, short on compassion.

A third man came up from the Jericho area to Jerusalem. This man came near the dying Jew. This man was the good Samaritan. He was a man of affirmative action.

Stirred by deep compassion, the Samaritan immediately went to where the man was dying. He knelt beside the beaten Jew, soothed his wounds with medicinal oil, and bandaged them. Then he put the wounded man on his donkey, took him to an inn, and nursed him throughout the night. Having to leave, the Samaritan paid the innkeeper to care for the man, promising to provide more money if it were needed.

This is the story of one wounded Jew, to whom all fellow Jews had some obligation. Yet the priest with all his strict do's and don'ts was emotionally impotent to help. The Levite with all his traditions was trapped in attractive emptiness.

But the Samaritan, not socially bound to help a Jew, was a man of affirmative action. A man of compassion, he was committed to meet the wounded man's needs. Because of his care the dying Jew lived.

There are many going down life's pathway who have been beaten by failure and bruised by betrayal. They are emotionally and spiritually near death. Some of these people are even our acquaintances and friends.

They do not need the law of do's and don'ts. They do not need the ritualism of empty traditions. But they do need friends who are willing to commit themselves, friends who speak words of positive confirmation, friends of affirmative action.

Forgiveness

No relationship is completely smooth and without difficulties. Moreover, it seems the closer a relationship becomes, the more the day-to-day hurts increase.

Unforgiven hurts are probably the greatest source of destruction to a relationship. If hurt is allowed to fester and seethe, it deepens. It puts up a barrier between two people that only forgiveness can break down. Even if a person is entirely justified in feeling hurt, nothing but harm can result if that hurt remains unforgiven.

There is an account given in the Bible of a paralyzed man. Some friends had brought him to Christ for healing. But Christ did not first go over to heal him. Instead He said to the paralyzed man, "Take heart, my son; your sins are forgiven" (Matt. 9:2, NEB). Perhaps this man's physical condition was caused by his need for forgiveness, for these words were followed by his healing. This story is a reminder to us: every time we allow hurts to remain unforgiven, we have caused relationships to be paralyzed.

The story of the wandering, or prodigal son is one of the most outstanding parables in the Bible. Scripture paints the picture of a loving father with two sons. All was well until one son decided he wanted to go his own way.

In the Orient this is a disgrace to the entire family. Instead of waiting for his father's death, he wanted his part of the family inheritance immediately. He selfishly took his newly acquired wealth and spent it freely on his own pleasures.

Eventually his money ran low. A famine swept the land, and he was reduced to feeding pigs—the lowest of all Hebrew occupations. Helpless and facing starvation, he decided to return home, composing a speech he hoped would trigger his father's forgiveness. His mind rang with the words: "Father, I have sinned against both heaven and you, and am no longer worthy to be called your son. Please take me on as a hired man." So he began the trip to his hometown. And while he was yet a long distance off his father saw him.

Now his father had been deeply hurt by the son's actions. In a sense the son's early desire for his inheritance was a desire for his father's death. We can imagine the villagers had spent long hours discussing the wandering son's wrongs and his father's great pain.

His father was a man of standing in the community. If he had waited for his son to come crawling to him in despair, and the father had let his anger bring the son to full repentance, that would have seemed the appropriate scene.

But the father deeply loved his son, like our heavenly Father loves us. Instead of making him endure the apprehension of that final walk home, instead of holding on to his dignity and pride, the father "was filled with loving pity and ran and embraced him and kissed him" (Luke 15:20, TLB).

The son tried to give his oft-practiced speech, but

did not even finish. There was no need. His father's forgiveness already flowed freely. The father ordered that his returned son have the finest robe, a jeweled ring and shoes.

"We must celebrate with a feast," the father said, "for this son of mine was dead and has returned to life. He was lost and is found" (Luke 15:23-24, TLB).

The father was committed to the son, desiring to fill his every need. He restored his son's self-image with words of confirmation. He followed his words with affirmative action.

Because of the father's forgiveness his relationship with his son could be fully restored. Any hurt, no matter how trivial it might seem, needs forgiveness. If we refuse to forgive, the particular relationship involved will be thwarted, and the building process delayed.

We must always be eagerly ready to forgive, yet never demanding forgiveness for ourselves. "Be gentle and ready to forgive; never hold grudges. Remember, the Lord forgave you, so you must forgive others" (Col. 3:13, TLB). Let us allow this injunction to forgive ring loud in our hearts, and let the healing power of forgiveness flow freely in our lives.

If you want to build a good relationship start with a solid foundation. Make sure you have an honest and faithful character of perseverance. Be certain you include God's provisions of an eternal relationship and an enduring hope.

Be careful to use the proper building materials. Build with commitment to meet the needs of others and to help them develop their best. Build with words of positive confirmation. Build with compassion in affirmative action. Build with a continual attitude of forgiveness. And above all, let Christ be the cornerstone.

Remember: God wants you to have full and enjoyable relationships. His resources are for your use. Take advantage of them, and enjoy a quality in relationships that you never thought possible!

7

Receiving Healing

At various points almost all of us have experienced sickness or disease. Often these periods of sickness are short, passing as we rest and allow our bodies the opportunity to recuperate.

There are, however, times when sickness lingers. There are incidents when human efforts provide no lasting relief. There are situations that need the healing touch of the Divine Physician.

Scripture records an interesting account: "Jesus returned to Jerusalem for one of the Jewish religious holidays. Inside the city, near the Sheep Gate, was Bethesda Pool, with five covered platforms or porches surrounding it. Crowds of sick folks—lame, blind, or with paralyzed limbs—lay on the platforms (waiting for a certain movement of the water, for an angel of the Lord came from time to time and disturbed the water, and the first person to step down into it afterwards was healed).

"One of the men lying there had been sick for thirty-eight years. When Jesus saw him and knew how long he had been ill, he asked him, 'Would you like to get well?'

" 'I can't,' the sick man said, 'for I have no one to help me into the pool at the movement of the water. While I am trying to get there, someone else always gets in ahead of me.'

"Jesus told him, 'Stand up, roll up your sleeping mat and go on home!'

"Instantly, the man was healed! He rolled up the mat and began walking!" (John 5:1-9, TLB).

When I read this account I marveled at God's mercy. But I also wondered why God had chosen to reveal His healing power at the Pool of Bethesda. After all, there were several other pools in Jerusalem, and the sick could be found nearly everywhere.

Then the Holy Spirit opened my inner eyes of understanding. He taught me that there were several reasons for God's choice, reasons that show how we, too, can receive healing. In the Greek *Bethesda* means "house of grace or mercy," healing being a grace God desires to bestow on His children of faith.

The Pool of Cleansing

It is significant that Bethesda was beside the sheep market. When a Jew wanted to worship God with a sacrifice for sin he first went to the sheep market.

After he selected and bought a sheep he first took the sheep to a nearby pool, the Pool of Bethesda. There he washed the sheep thoroughly, so it would be clean. He did this for a reason. God would not accept a dirty sheep as a sacrifice: it had to be without spot or blemish of any kind.

David said that we were all born in sin: "I was born a sinner, yes, from the moment my mother conceived me" (Ps. 51:5, TLB). If we are to be accepted by God, we also must be washed. But our pool of cleansing is different.

Christ lived a sinless life—without spot or blemish. He came and took our sins and sicknesses upon himself, and carried them to the cross. With His death on the cross Jesus Christ shed His blood for us. It is only by His shed blood that we are washed and cleansed from all sin. The blood of Jesus has become our Pool of Bethesda.

It only takes simple faith in Jesus Christ to wash in God's cleansing pool. Even now the Holy Spirit can apply the blood of Jesus to your heart and make you clean. If you are cleansed by the blood of Jesus then you are freed from the guilt of sin. If you are cleansed by the blood of Christ then you can boldy approach God in prayer, certain that He will hear your request for healing.

The Cleansing Pool: A Step to Sacrifice
The sheep that were washed at the pool were soon

to be sacrificed on the altar. Do you need a miracle in your body? Do you want the power of the Holy Spirit to come into your life? Do you want God to hear your prayers? Then, as a blood-washed child of God, you must place your life as a sacrifice on the altar of God.

This is not an easy step to take. But God cannot fully heal you unless you become a sacrifice unto Him. When you sacrifice your life completely to God, He will open the doors of heaven and pour out His blessings upon you.

Near the Pool: The Persistent and Patient

In our world today the emphasis is on action. Everything moves fast: go, go, go! Hurry, hurry, hurry!

Even when we come to church we often expect God to answer us immediately.

"God," we pray, "heal me. You know how much I hurt and suffer. You have all the power in the universe, so please heal me now."

Then we open our eyes and expect that God has immediately healed us. If He has not we are deeply disappointed, and often angry. But with that kind of attitude God can never do anything for us. God wants us to take time with Him. He wants us to patiently and persistently wait for His divine purposes to unfold.

The people at the Pool of Bethesda were persistent. They waited patiently for the water to stir. In the same way that the water of the Pool of Bethesda was stirred by an angel, we must wait until our hearts are stirred by the Holy Spirit.

When the Water Was Stirred

During commonplace days the people waiting by the Bethesda Pool used its water to wash their faces. It was only ordinary water. But when the angel came and stirred that water it became a miracle-producing pool.

Many people come to church and simply listen to the words of a sermon. Often the words of a sermon refer only to a general knowledge of the Bible, a knowledge accessible to anyone who will hear or read it. This word and knowledge has been referred to as *logos.*

In a passage in Romans a different shade of meaning can be seen: "Yet faith comes from listening to this Good News—the Good News about Christ" (Rom. 10:17, TLB). Here the word *rhema* is used: a specific word to a specific person in a specific situation. Although there is truth in *logos,* it is *rhema* that brings the faith that sparks us to fruitful action, that gives the faith needed for healing.

When you read the Bible you are reading *logos.* After you meditate on the Word, some portion or portions of Scripture will seem to stand out to you. As the Holy Spirit stirs your heart, *logos* turns into *rhema,* and becomes a specific word to you in a specific situation.

The *rhema* of God's Word will spur you to active belief. Just as the waters of Bethesda were stirred so will those portions of Scripture move your heart. Then, and only then, can you experience a miracle.

One Cold Winter Night

Distinct in my memory is an incident that took place about twenty years ago, in the beginning of my ministry. One Sunday I went to the tent church where we were holding services. As I preached the morning message I realized I could not feel God's presence. While I preached I shuddered and stammered, and many in the congregation fell asleep.

After that Sunday morning service I wanted to resign from my church. I wondered if God had truly called me into the ministry. Having lost my appetite I could not eat lunch. I prayed instead, preparing for the evening service. I wanted that service to be a great success.

But the evening service was even worse than the morning service. I was rapidly growing to hate myself.

Although it was a cold winter night I could not go to bed. I wrapped myself in a blanket, sat in the chilling tent church, and prayed. Feeling deeply depressed, it seemed to me that even my prayers could do no good.

Suddenly I heard a sound. A young crippled man with badly injured knees came crawling to where I sat. I thought he had come to beg for money.

"Where is the pastor?" he asked.

"I am the pastor."

"Well," he confessed, "I came to be healed."

I could not even preach a decent sermon. How could I pray for someone in his condition?

"Where are you from?" I inquired.

"I was begging at the Seoul railroad station. Then a man invited me to your church. He told me you would pray for me, and I would be healed."

I tried to find some excuse: "You are not even a Christian. God could never heal a sinner."

"How can I become a Christian?" he returned.

I then explained to him God's plan of salvation. He began to call upon the name of Jesus, and was miraculously saved. His life was cleansed in Christ's Pool of Bethesda.

"Sir, I am ready," he entreated. His words and attitudes expressed a complete sacrifice. He willingly laid everything on God's altar of submission.

I prepared to pray for him. But so severe was the injury to his knees that I questioned whether Christ himself could heal them. I laid my hand on him and tried to pray, but could hardly open my mouth. "Father," I mumbled quietly, "in the name of Jesus, heal this young man."

Faithless, I directed the young man, "Try to stand up." Then I helped him, only to find his legs dangling like those of a puppet.

"Sit down here," I ordered him. "I'll go and get some more faith."

Approaching the altar at the front of the church, I began to pray. But though I was persistent, my prayers were filled with words of complaint, not petition: "God, why did you send this man to my church? You know I can't help him. You must supply me with more faith."

I then began to repeat all the Scriptures about healing that I could remember. But these Scriptures were just words, *logos,* to me. Although I could sense nothing different, I turned to the young man.

"Let's try once again." I laid my hand on him, saying: "Be healed in the name of Jesus!"

I took him by the hand, "Now let's try to stand up."

Once again his legs just dangled.

"Please, sit back down."

I returned to the altar, praying: "Lord, if you don't supply faith to me, I would rather just sit here and die."

Then for hours I sat there in prayer, thinking about the Holy Spirit and waiting upon the Lord. This young man and I had much in common: he was crippled with an injury, and I was crippled with doubt. But now we were both among the patient and persistent, waiting for the Holy Spirit to stir the waters.

Suddenly I could sense God's Spirit come upon me in a special way. As the angel had stirred the water at the Pool of Bethesda, so my heart was being stirred by the Holy Spirit. My faith began to increase. *Logos* became *rhema,* and I almost felt as if I could move the earth. When I turned to look at the young crippled man, his healing no longer seemed an impossibility. I stood up and started to approach him once again.

Three Thieves Frightened

At that same moment three thieves came in the church to steal anything of value. "You," I said pointing to them, "come and take hold of this man. I am going to pray for him to be healed."

Curious, they obeyed. Then I stood on the young man's knees and prayed, "In the name of Jesus, be whole."

I then jumped to the side. The bones in his knees began to crack. Bewildered, the young man started to cry, "Help! This man is killing me."

Frightened, the thieves ran away.

When I helped the young man up his legs still dangled. But my faith was strong. Taking firm hold of him, I commanded, "In the name of Jesus, walk!"

Then I gave him a slight shove, and closed my eyes. I was afraid to see what would happen.

Soon I heard a noise. When I opened my eyes I saw that young man, full of healthy vitality, running around the whole area. The three thieves came back and saw what God had done in that young man's life. Crying out, they asked for God's forgiveness.

The next Sunday a prominent doctor came to the church, and publicly testified that God had healed the crippled young man. That doctor became a Christian, and later served as an elder in my church. Those three former thieves went to Bible college, and are now outstanding ministers in Korea.

The Living God

Christ is more than a religion, more than an institution, more than a system of ethics. He is the living God!

Like the man in Scripture who suffered for thirty-eight years you may have seen many miracles take place around you. The sick man had often seen the water troubled by the angel of God, but had no one to help him into the pool.

Then Jesus came into his life. Christ told him to rise up and walk. Christ focused on his point of need, and confronted him with the opportunity for healing. The *rhema* words of Christ stirred this man's heart, and he was given faith. Jesus performed the miracle he needed, and this man became whole.

Healing Available

Christ showed us that we need no longer journey to Jerusalem and sit around the Pool of Bethesda to be healed. God wants to do the same thing He did for the sick man near the pool—for you.

You may go to church and listen to the same sermons again and again, yet not experience anything. But if you have the ultimate miracle of salvation, wait upon the Lord and seek after God. Let your life be a living sacrifice to God, filled with submission to the unfolding of God's purposes. Become one of the patient and persistent.

One day God's Word will become like stirred holy water to your heart. *Logos* will become specific *rhema*, and God will pour His faith out to you. When this happens in faith make your request for healing known to God. Then you must wake fully from your slumber, take up your sleeping mat of hesitance, and walk boldly!

8

Living with Persistent Perplexity

The Apostle Paul's life was filled with evidence of God's supernatural power. He even went to heaven once. His account of that experience reads: "Fourteen years ago I was taken up to heaven for a visit. Don't ask me whether my body was there or just my spirit, for I don't know; only God can answer that. But . . . there I was in paradise, and heard things so astounding that they are beyond a man's power to describe or put in words" (2 Cor. 12:2-4, TLB).

In the city of Lystra, the Apostle Paul had been instrumental in the healing of a crippled man who had been lame from birth. Later, self-righteous Jews came to Lystra, inciting the crowds to harm Paul. The people began to stone Paul. Thinking that he was dead, the people then dragged Paul outside the city to the area where the dead were taken to be disposed. Believers then encircled Paul, praying for him. Suddenly Paul was resuscitated, and brought fully back to life.

Paul was a believer who had gone through much difficulty: "Five different times the Jews gave me their terrible thirty-nine lashes. Three times I was beaten with rods. Once I was stoned. Three times I was ship-wrecked. Once I was in the open sea all night and the whole next day. I have traveled many weary miles and have been often in great danger from flooded rivers, and from robbers, and from my own people, the Jews, as well as from the hands of the Gentiles" (2 Cor. 11:24-26a, TLB).

Paul suffered much because of his belief and faith in Christ. Yet it was Paul who wrote books that were to eloquently tell of God's goodness: "For I am convinced that nothing can ever separate us from his love. Death can't, and life can't. The angels won't, and all the powers of hell itself cannot keep God's love away. Our fears for today, our worries about tomorrow, or where we are—high above the sky, or in the deepest ocean—nothing will ever be able to separate us from the love of God demonstrated by our Lord Jesus Christ when he died for us" (Rom. 8:38-39, TLB).

When reading Romans and Galatians the reader is amazed at the tremendous depth of revelation Paul expounds. Many believers felt that salvation was attained by keeping the law. But in his letters Paul clearly shows that after the death of Christ on the cross, salvation comes solely by faith in God's finished work. The Apostle Paul left a legacy that enriches our lives, even today. The Apostle Paul is to many of us believers the example of what every Christian should be like.

But there is one thing we sometimes tend to forget: God allowed Paul "a thorn in the flesh." Though Paul begged and prayed to God three times to remove this thorn, God refused, replying, " 'My grace is all you need; power comes to its full strength in weakness' " (2 Cor. 12:9, NEB).

God allowed that thorn, a messenger of Satan, to harass Paul continually. God did not want Paul to become enveloped in thinking of himself and his marvelous revelations or difficult experiences. God did not want Paul buried in memories of the past. God wanted Paul to depend on the Lord Jesus Christ for daily sustenance. God allowed Paul to live with that thorn, that persistent perplexity, in order that Christ's power be perpetually evident in his life.

Just as God allowed Paul a thorn in the flesh, a persistent perplexity, so does God sometimes allow persistent perplexities in our lives. God never wants us to fall into casual comfort. He wants us to continue to seek after Him, to continue to develop our faith lives, to continue to make Him the focal point of our thoughts and dreams. This is why God will not bind Satan and cast him into hell now. God allows Satan to buffet us so that we will not become lazy or complacent in our relationship with the Lord. For this reason persistent perplexities have been termed "the thorn of grace."

Yet when the perplexities persist, when the thorn

comes and pricks us, we often complain. If we could, however, look into the future we would see that this in reality is a tremendous blessing from God. If we will but let them, persistent perplexities can be God's provision of grace for a successful Christian life.

Some perplexities persist for a short while, others remain throughout our lives. For the purpose of further exploration let us consider Paul's thorn—Paul's persistent perplexity—symbolically, and focus in on the types of perplexity that can persist in our lives.

The Perplexity of Weakness

Weakness can take many forms: physical, emotional, social, mental, or spiritual. Though God could remove the perplexity of weakness from our lives, He sometimes chooses to allow it to remain. Though weakness, like a thorn, brings us discomfort, it can also bring us into a deeper dimension in our Christian walk.

Through His death and resurrection Jesus not only took away our sins, but He also carried away our sicknesses, our physical weaknesses. We have as much right and authority to claim healing from our illnesses as we do claim forgiveness of our sins. Yet there are times God allows our sicknesses to linger, for in those particular situations He has a greater plan for us than restoration of our health.

I have experienced this personally. In 1964 I was a young minister with several thousand members in my church. I began to think I was one of God's accomplished servants, and I almost entered into a complacency in my ministry.

Then God allowed the perplexity of physical weakness to be my thorn. I developed a case of nervous exhaustion and some problems with my heart. From that moment on I was newly forced to depend upon the strength of Christ, even to simply carry out my daily tasks. During my recuperation God had the time and opportunity to show me many changes that needed to take place in my life, my ministry, and my church.

At that point I questioned God's wisdom in letting sickness cripple my life's activities. But after God had made the needed changes a part of my modified mentality, the perplexity of weakness was lifted. I regained strength and the power to institute the needed changes. My life, ministry, and church have never been the same since. All three reached heights I had only dreamed about before.

The Perplexity of Rejection

Paul knew the perplexity of rejection. He visited many towns where his own fellow Jews cast him out. Paul wrote: "I have met dangers from rivers, dangers from robbers, dangers from my fellow-countrymen, dangers from foreigners . . . dangers from false friends" (2 Cor. 11:26, NEB). It was because of the accusation of fellow Jews that Paul was kept in chains, destined for an early death.

We, too, sometimes face the perplexity of rejection.

The acceptance of our friends and associates grows thin; the thorn of rejection will on occasion persist, a perplexity whose disappearance we deeply desire.

But these are not times for despair, but rather for learning. Like Paul we should learn not to depend on the praise and support of any man. We should only seek after the approval of God.

The Perplexity of Persecution

Persecution is a perplexity that has persisted in many believers' lives. Vivid in our memories are the stories of Jewish Christians in the terrifying concentration camps of Germany during the war. During the Korean War persecution of Christians was also frequent, with death seeming to many a welcome end.

The persecution in our lives is rarely so pronounced. We often encounter a more subtle kind of persecution: the refusal of a friendship with an unbeliever, the upturned nose of one who balks at our belief, neighbors who tempt us to anger just to watch and muse over our reactions. For some, persecution of any sort is a rare occurrence; for others it is a constant reality.

Paul's persecutions caused him to be a lonely man. He—like the Jewish Christians in Germany during the war, like the Christians in Korea during the war—realized a desperate need to welcome and feel the presence of God in his life and heart. He realized more fully his need for God's companionship, comfort, and strength. The perplexity of persecution is a thorn-prick that guides us to complete reliance on the never-changing Christ.

The Perplexity of Hardship

Hardship is another of God's thorns of grace. Hardship refers to the difficulties of life that cause us discomfort, poverty, pain, unrealized or thwarted expectations. Hardship also involves calamity—extreme misfortunes or disasters that bring us misery.

Joseph's life was filled with the perplexity of hardship. Because he was favored by his father, he was sold to traders by his brothers. Slave of the palace guard Potiphar, Joseph refused the invitation of Potiphar's wife to an immoral affair, and was thrown into prison. The perplexity of hardship remained a persistent theme through that portion of Joseph's life. But he learned a lesson that was to be vital in the events ahead: He learned to rely on God's grace and he learned that God was faithful, even in the midst of hardship.

The story of Joseph shows the result of his perplexity of hardship. He became governor of all Egypt. Because of Joseph's wisdom the famine in Egypt caused minimal harm, and he was able to provide food to keep his family and people from starvation.

God is the same yesterday, today and forever. The God who dealt with Paul is dealing with you. If you have thorns of persistent perplexity in your life do not be discouraged. Whether yours is the perplexity of weakness, of rejection, of persecution, or of hardship, determine never to leave the presence of the Lord. His grace is all we need; through our inadequacies, frustrations and weaknesses Christ's power can shine forth.

Do not despair about the perplexities that persist in your life. Learn by them. Recognize your own inabilities, and lean on God's strength. Spend time in prayer. And let the grace of our Lord Jesus Christ make you a person of beauty.

9

Destroying Deception

One of man's basic quests is a quest for truth. But all around the problem of deception looms large. Moreover, before truth can be discovered, deception must be destroyed.

Christians are engaged in a continual spiritual war of emancipation. One of their primary tasks is the destruction of deception. Unbelievers live under the bondage of Satan, suffering from the curse and from death since the time of Adam. We are not only responsible to destroy the deception around ourselves; we are also obligated to fight in order to set others free from deception.

A key to the destruction of deception is found in God's Word, the Bible: "The weapons we wield are not merely human, but divinely potent to demolish strongholds" (2 Cor. 10:4, NEB). If the strongholds of deception are to be destroyed, divine weapons must be used—weapons of permanent power, not of temporary strength.

The passage reads on, to give the threefold manner in which deception can be eradicated: "Casting down imaginations, and every high thing that exalteth itself against the knowledge of God, and bringing into captivity every thought to the obedience of Christ" (2 Cor. 10:5, KJV). In these three ways deception can be destroyed.

Cast Down Imaginations

One way to fight against the deceptions of Satan is to cast down imaginations, human reasonings. One version of the Bible terms imaginations as "proud arguments" (TLB), and another calls them "sophistries" (NEB)—subtle and superficially believable, but generally false methods of reasoning. If you and I are to destroy deception we must cast down imaginations, break down proud arguments, and demolish sophistries.

When you read in Genesis about the lives of Adam and Eve in the Garden of Eden, you can perceive the beginning of the deceptions of Satan. In the Garden Adam and Eve were permitted to eat all kinds of wonderful food except one: the fruit of the tree in the center of the Garden, the tree of the knowledge of good and evil. God told them that they were forbidden to eat from this one tree, "You may eat from every tree in the garden, but not from the tree of the knowledge of good and evil; for on the day that you eat from it, you will certainly die" (Gen. 2:16-17, NEB).

In one sense the tree of knowledge of good and evil was the fruit of reasoning. God had, and still has, absolute authority. His commands must be obeyed unconditionally, without using human reasoning concerning good and evil.

When Satan entered the Garden of Eden, he maneuvered in such a way that God's command became the object of imaginations, of reasonings of good and evil. The story in Genesis points this out.

"The serpent was the craftiest of all the creatures the Lord God had made. So the serpent came to the woman. 'Really?' he asked. '*None* of the fruit in the garden? God says you mustn't eat *any* of it?'

" 'Of course we may eat it,' the woman told him. 'It's only the fruit from the tree at the *center* of the garden that we are not to eat. God says we mustn't eat it or even touch it, or we will die.'

" 'That's a lie!' the serpent hissed. 'You'll not die! God knows very well that the instant you eat it you will become like him, for your eyes will be opened—you will be able to distinguish good from evil!' " (Gen. 3:1-5, TLB).

Man-centered reasonings of good and evil require that man's position before God change from that of a created being to that of an independent being. If man views God's commands with just his own measure of good and evil he is asserting himself to be equal with his Creator, on God's same level of thinking and decision-making. In reality this is rebellion. Satan attempted to bring God's Word to the point of argument before Eve. But God's Word should never be argued. God's commands must be carried out in detail.

This is where Adam and Eve made a great mistake. They put the Word of God on the level of discussion and argument. As a result, they were deceived, and ate of the fruit of the tree of knowledge of good and evil. And in those bites of rebellion they were declaring their independence from and their equality with God. It is impossible for a created being to be equal with its creator; but because of the deception of Satan, this is what Adam and Eve attempted to do.

Because they acted on the basis of their imaginations, of their human reasonings, they broke their trust with God, committing a sin that brought separation. Instead of casting down imaginations they allowed deception to dwell in their minds, and they were cast out of the Garden of Eden.

In essence the story of King Saul in the Old Testament is the story of imaginations that were allowed to have precedence, the story of the rebellion of human reasonings. Saul was given a clear command from God. The nation of Amalek had attacked the Israelites when they had been traveling up from Egypt. God was now going to avenge their evil, and commanded Saul to "completely destroy the entire Amalek nation," (1 Sam. 15:3, TLB), each and every person, as well as all the livestock.

But Saul had his own ideas. Although he killed every

person, he spared the king as a showpiece, and was negligent in carrying out the full command: "Saul and his men kept the best of the sheep and oxen and the fattest of the lambs—everything, in fact, that appealed to them. They destroyed only what was worthless or of poor quality" (1 Sam. 15:9, TLB).

Samuel, one of God's chosen prophets, found out what Saul had done, and confronted him with his misdeeds: " 'Why," asked Samuel, 'didn't you obey the Lord? Why did you rush for the loot and do exactly what God said not to?'

" 'But I *have* obeyed the Lord,' Saul insisted. 'I did what he told me to do; and I brought King Agag but killed everyone else. And it was only when my troops demanded it that I let them keep the best of the sheep and oxen and loot to sacrifice to the Lord' " (1 Sam. 15:19-21, TLB).

Samuel replied to Saul's deception, " 'Has the Lord as much pleasure in your burnt offerings and sacrifices as in your obedience? Obedience is far better than sacrifice. He is much more interested in your listening to him than in your offering the fat of rams to him. For rebellion is as bad as the sin of witchcraft, and stubbornness is as bad as worshiping idols. And now because you have rejected the word of Jehovah, he has rejected you from being king' " (1 Sam. 15:22-23, TLB).

King Saul had not accepted God's command as an absolute. He had accepted God's command according to his own imaginations and reasonings, his own understanding of good and evil, with respect to his benefit and thinking.

We tend to do this same thing. Like King Saul and like Adam and Eve, we sift God's commandments—ultimate truth—through our own understanding of good and evil. We analyze God's truths in the light of our imaginations, our own reasoning power. We argue with God, wanting to be independent and equal with Him.

But human imaginations, human reasonings of good and evil, only block the truth. If deception is to be destroyed, these proud arguments with God must be cast down.

Faith is an important element in this casting down. As your faith in God grows and deepens, your arguments against God lessen. As your human reasonings—imaginations—decrease, you can live more intimately with God, and Satan has less opportunity to continue deceiving you, to continue blocking you from the truth.

So let us cast down our imaginations, our human reasonings. Let us obey God's commands without question, casting down our own imaginations. Let us allow the truth of God to shine forth.

Cast Down Every High Thing

We can also destroy deception by "casting down . . . every high thing that exalteth itself against the knowledge of God" (2 Cor. 10:5). This has been termed "all that rears its proud head against the knowledge of God" (2 Cor. 10:5, NEB), forming the foundation for a deception that is brazenly against God, against divine truth.

The building of the Tower of Babel portrayed this kind of deception. God's stance with the people of the earth at this time was good. After the flood God promised: "As long as the earth remains, there will be springtime and harvest, cold and heat, winter and summer, day and night" (Gen. 8:22, TLB). God followed this promise of perpetual continuity with a clear set of directions: "Have many children and repopulate the earth and subdue it." (Gen. 9:7, TLB).

But the people rebelled against the plan of God: "At that time all mankind spoke a single language. As the population grew and spread eastward, a plain was discovered in the land of Babylon, and was soon thickly populated. The people who lived there began to talk about building a great city, with a temple-tower reaching to the skies—a proud, eternal monument to themselves.

" 'This will weld us together,' they said, 'and keep us from scattering all over the world.' So they made great piles of hard-burned brick, and collected bitumen to use as mortar" (Gen. 11:1-4, TLB).

Notice their intentions to build a "proud, eternal monument to themselves," to "keep us from scattering all over the world." Their deception arose out of a desire for a proud, eternal monument to themselves.

They raised their own recognition above their recognition of God.

God had directed them to scatter and repopulate the earth. But they wanted the opposite: to band and cleave together, a group of self-satisfied, self-made gods.

In the face of their deception God was forced to act. He gave them different languages, causing them confusion, a confusion that lead to the name of their city—Babel. With their languages diverse, and their understanding confused, the building project of the temple-tower was halted. And soon they began to scatter more, using common language groups as points of unity.

This same type of occurrence has happened repeatedly. When we try to exalt ourselves high above God, we become part of a deception that must be confused and halted.

Language is the vehicle of ideas and ideologies. Around our present world there are multiplied ideologies—communism, capitalism, neutralism, humanism. Humanity is being confused, just as people were at the Tower of Babel, because it has tried to elevate itself to be equal with God, disobeying God's commands. For this reason God has allowed a spirit of confusion to take hold of the world today.

The destruction of the Roman Empire also exemplifies this type of deception. The Roman religious hierarchy became a spiritual Tower of Babel. Then God caused this great empire to become confused. It was divided into the eastern and western empires that were finally destroyed by the invasions of barbarians.

Other civilizations also have had this destructive deception within them. The historian Toynbee wrote that during the twentieth century more than twenty civilizations have risen and fallen. Every high thing that exalts itself against the knowledge of God must be cast down.

Captive Thoughts

A third way we can destroy deception is by bringing "into captivity every thought to the obedience of Christ" (2 Cor. 10:5). There is an important truth lodged in these words. If you capture someone's thoughts you have captured that person.

Think how the commercial world uses mass communication. Turn on the television or radio, and look at a newspaper. All around you see advertisements. This is the age of advertising, and all over our society is flooded with advertisements.

Recently my three sons were watching television when they saw a commercial about a new kind of instant noodle. Then they approached my wife, "Mama, there's a new kind of noodle now. Please buy us some."

When I returned home from church my second son rushed into the kitchen, clutching a package of those new noodles. "Papa," he exclaimed, "look at this! We are eating noodles just like they show on television."

Through constant advertisement the business world

captures the thoughts and imaginations of the public. Indirectly and subconsciously, the public—you and me—is being controlled through mass communications. We think we are deciding things independently, according to our own desires. But this is not true.

We are constantly maneuvered by the business world, a world continually feeding propaganda into our subconscious thoughts. We cease making decisions according to our own desires, but rather according to the desires prompted by advertisements. Heretics and communists use the same thought-captivating tactics. They brainwash people's minds, making them slaves to their ideologies and demands.

Only when our thoughts become captive to Jesus Christ can we destroy deception fully. Only then will we be able to have the freedom of truth. Jesus Christ himself is ultimate truth, bringing to us life, freedom and blessings.

To destroy deception and enjoy freedom in divine truth your thoughts must be captured into obedience to Christ. Try to absorb the thoughts of Jesus into your mind. Imprint them in your mind by studying God's Word. Read and meditate on the Bible diligently, and let it become a part of your thinking process. Attend church faithfully, and listen carefully to the sermons and teachings given.

Ask the Holy Spirit to help you. Remember that "those who let themselves be controlled by their lower natures live only to please themselves," remaining and wallowing in deception. But "those who follow after the Holy Spirit find themselves doing those things that please God" (Rom. 8:5, TLB). They learn how to destroy deception by bringing their thoughts captive into obedience to Christ. If we are to be free to enjoy divine truth we, too, must let our thoughts be captive to Christ.

God is author of all truth. Divine truth is available to us in God's Word, the Bible. But before that truth can become a reality to us, deception must be destroyed. To destroy deception, imaginations, human reasonings of good and evil, must be cast down. To destroy deception, every high thing raised to be equal to God—whether it be an ambition, an idea, or an aspiration—must be cast down. To destroy deception every thought needs to become captive to the obedience of Christ. Only when deception is destroyed can we cease the struggles in our quest for truth. Only then can you and I completely enjoy the life, peace and blessings that truth in Christ brings.

10

Overcoming Difficulty

Nature's storms are frequent occurrences. Although we do not want them, storms, tornadoes, and hurricanes do come. They leave behind the devastation of disordered houses, ruined crops, and uprooted lives.

Just as we have natural storms, we also have spiritual, mental and relational storms. Trials, troubles and difficulties come into our lives, threatening to leave behind a path of disrupted hopes, unrealized ambitions, and unmet expectations. These uninvited storms come more than once into our lives as Christians. And there is no exception: we all experience the storms of difficulty.

When your life becomes overshadowed by a black cloud of foreboding difficulty, you may suffer terrible destruction if you do not know how to deal with it. But there is a solution. Through following the example and attitudes of the Apostle Paul in Acts 27, we can be overcomers. We can be victorious.

Listen to the Right Voices

Because he had been preaching the gospel of Christ, Paul was traveling as one of the chained prisoners on a ship. During the journey Paul and other prisoners were placed in the custody of an officer named Julius. They stopped at the harbor of Fair Havens on the Island of Crete, and stayed for several days.

The weather grew worse, and winter was soon to set in. Because Fair Havens was an exposed harbor it was a poor place to spend the winter. Most of the crew felt it would be better to proceed to Phoenicia, and winter there. They listened to the voice of human reason, and let it guide their decision.

Paul heard a different voice, the voice of God. At this juncture Paul gave an important warning: " 'Sirs,' he said, 'I believe there is trouble ahead if we go on— perhaps shipwreck, loss of cargo, injuries, and death' " (Acts 27:10, TLB).

But the crew was indifferent to what Paul had to say. They listened to the voice of reason, and destined themselves to disaster.

The Bible clearly shows two contrasting voices speaking to us today. One is from above, and the other is bound by the limits of the earth. When you read the Bible and when you go to church and hear God's Word preached, you are hearing the voice from the world above. But once you enter the temporal world you are flooded with the voice of earthly temptation, the voice from the world of Satan. As the crew of Paul's ship was forced to make a decision, so are you. And if you do not listen to the right voice, unfavorable results are unavoidable.

Many difficult problems loom like mountains, seeming too large to be solved. Technological and scientific developments abound, but we still lack the wisdom to make sound decisions and live successful lives.

Paul's words were truth in his particular situation. The Bible is truth for all ages. It has the resources of God's abundant wisdom and knowledge. Through the Bible, the voice from above clearly speaks, providing warnings of wisdom to all who are encountering difficulties.

Yet many neglect reading the Bible. "Oh," they remark, "the Bible belongs to antiquity. It is not for today." I feel sorry for such people. Their modern scientific knowledge and reason can never replace the wisdom contained in the Word of God. Through biblical teaching, God clearly shows us we must make our daily decisions based on His infallible Word, and not on the voices of fallible human reason alone.

From now on when you have a difficult problem read and meditate on the Word of God. Go to God in prayer, and listen to the voice that will lead you into an everlasting life of love.

Realize Your Restrictions
In the beginning it looked like it was going to be a

beautiful trip. The weather seemed perfect, the prisoners well-behaved, and much merchandise was on
board.

Then as they sailed through the Aegean Sea, the
weather abruptly changed. A storm with heavy winds
of typhoon strength overtook them. The ship was
caught in the middle of this storm, pushed further out
to sea, and tossed about helplessly.

On the first day of the storm they "banded the ship
with ropes to strengthen the hull" (Acts 27:17, TLB).
On the second day the storm was so severe and the
waves so boisterous that they knew they were at the
mercy of their difficulty. They sorrowfully began to
throw all the cargo into the sea, intending to lighten
the ship. This act ended all their hopes of monetary
profit. At that point they were fighting for their very
lives.

The storm continued a third day, and the seas grew
higher. As a last resort they threw out the ship's tackle,
an act that meant they could no longer control the ship.
The situation was beyond their control and their only
respite was hope.

But the storm's winds did not lessen. The rolling sea
became worse and worse. "The terrible storm raged
unabated many days, until at last all hope was gone"
(Acts 27:20, TLB). And such is the plight of human
wisdom when faced by a storm of difficulty.

I have been preaching for more than twenty years,
meeting many people passing through life's storms.

For a while they try to do as the people on the ship. They try to support their homes, businesses and personal lives through their own wisdom, determination and experience. For a short time they feel as if they can make it.

However, they soon find that their own wisdom cannot control their situations. They then start lightening their ships of life. They start giving up their hopes, their profits, and even their positions.

This still does not carry their ships of life safely through. After all their hopes are exhausted they become desperate. They become aware of the restricted confines of their own abilities. It is then that many go to God, asking for divine help.

We humans seem strong and self-confident when everything is going smoothly. But when the stormy winds of difficulty begin to flow in our lives our faith in human wisdom and technology weakens. We are not a match for the storms that come into our lives. We must realize our restrictions. We must be continually ready to call on God, and receive help and wisdom from above.

The Certainty of "Belonging-ness"

When the passengers and crew gave up hope, they became forlorn, and even stopped eating. Paul, however, reacted differently. He knew how to overcome life's storms.

In a portion of Paul's discourse to his shipmates we

find three important secrets in surmounting difficulties. In telling those aboard about the visit of an angel Paul first declared "the God to whom I belong" (Acts 27:23, TLB).

For the people who belong to God, God is their heritage. We Christians should not look to the world, money, fame or human ingenuity. Our resource is from God. God is our bank, God is our life, God is our business, and God is our success.

When Christ died on the cross He did not leave any tangible assets for His followers. He did not leave land, money or position. But He did leave His followers the most wonderful of all heritages. He opened the way to restored relationship with our Father God, Creator of heaven and earth. Through Jesus Christ God becomes our heritage, our tremendous prize. Once God becomes our heritage, we need no longer look to the world or to human ingenuity to help us; God's resources become our own. We belong to God, and in that certainty we believe God will see us through any difficulty we encounter.

I read a story of one poor minister's wife. Her husband had a part-time job while he pioneered a small church. Their life was full of poverty; they could barely make ends meet each month. Then her husband lost his job. Because the church was so small their salary from it was limited to a token. Bills continued to pile up, but they had no funds to pay them. They did not know what to do.

The wife then went out and found a job. But it did not provide enough to meet their needs. One day, out of desperation, the minister's wife started reading the Bible. Her eyes fell on a passage in the book of Matthew. Recorded in that passage was the incident in Capernaum when the temple tax collectors approached Peter, asking him if Christ paid the temple tax. Paul immediately responded, "Of course He does."

When Peter came to Jesus, Jesus asked him, "Do kings levy assessments against their own people, or against conquered foreigners?"

"Against the foreigners," replied Peter.

Christ then said that they were supposed to be exempt. "However, we don't want to offend them, so go down to the shore and throw in a line, and open the mouth of the first fish you catch. You will find a coin to cover the taxes for both of us; take it and pay them" (Matt. 17:25-27, TLB).

The poor minister's wife was deeply impressed with this Scripture. The portion that particularly pointed to her predicament was where Christ showed Peter how to pay the taxes "for both of us." She realized she belonged to Christ, and that He belonged to her. Her life and Christ's were not two lives, but one.

Moved by the realization of the certainty of her "belonging-ness," she began to cry. She later shared the truth of this passage with her husband. She told her husband, "We are living together with Christ. Christ can find the source of funds to meet our needs."

Full of faith, they began to pray together. Soon after, God answered. The husband found a wonderful job. They were able to pay all their debts. They later became successful pioneer ministers, and their church grew large.

Through her experience the minister's wife discovered she belonged to God. The certainty of this realization brought powerful results. Paul also knew—despite tempestuous storm winds and forlorn hope—that he belonged to God.

People without belief in Christ have no place of true solution to turn to when things go wrong, when the storms of life threaten devastation, when the whole world seems angry. But we Christians know we belong to God. We know God is our heritage and our protector. Even if the entire earth becomes our enemy we have the unshakable rock of Christ, to stand upon. For we belong to God and God belongs to us.

The Trust in Service

Paul also declared a "God . . . whom I serve" (Acts 27:23, TLB). Paul exemplified to us a second secret in surmounting difficulties: that we should cast our cares on Christ, Son of the never-changing God who will never betray our trust. We all serve either God, or our own desires. Those desires are often a willing instrument of sin, a portion of the world infamous for the convenience of betrayal.

When most people are young and strong they serve

the world of their own desires. They think this world will continue to support them, and continue to give them the security of personal pleasure. Sooner of later, though, this world betrays them. Their youth disappears, and they become the fragile and trembling elderly.

Trust in money, and money will fail you. Trust in your position, and you will lose it. Trust in power, and it will leave you. Trust in fame, and it will elude you. But trust in God, and He will never fail you.

Christ lived a life of service. Jesus was born in a manger amidst poverty; He wanted to be a friend to the lonely. Because of our sins He took to the cross; God himself left Christ. For a short while Jesus cried from the cross: "My God, why have you forsaken me?"; He wanted to be a friend to the brokenhearted. Jesus tasted death, and was resurrected; He wanted to be a friend to those in need of everlasting life and peace.

If Jesus is your Lord, the same attitude of service is in you. You will want to serve God; He wants to serve you. Even though you might be poor, even though you might be lonely, even though you might be brokenhearted, and even though you might taste death, God will never leave you. He remains your friend through everything you experience.

Paul knew this. Although passing through a tempestuous storm, Paul knew Jesus was passing through it with him. In the middle of tragedy Paul could stand and declare that he served God. Because Paul served God,

God sent him an angel, a divine messenger with a promise of deliverance: "God has granted your request and will save the lives of all those sailing with you" (Acts 27:23, TLB).

If you faithfully serve God with your money, your time, your life, and your talents, then when difficulties come, God will send His angel to help you. God will be with you not only during the good times, but also when you pass through the dark storms of your life. Even if the world forsakes you completely God's trust remains eternal.

The Power of Promise

Through His angel, God made Paul a promise. When Paul declared his faith in that promise, he unleashed a power that brought it to fruition: "So take courage! For I believe God! It will be just as he said!" (Acts 27:25, TLB). The power of God's promise is the third secret Paul exemplified for us during the tempestuous storm.

God is almighty. He is the Creator of heaven and earth. God cannot lie for He is truth. Once God speaks it will be done. You can therefore put your complete faith in God's Word, the Bible. You therefore need to continually read the Bible, and ask the Holy Spirit to show you the promises God would make alive in your circumstances. In every situation ask that God's Holy Spirit take a promise from the Bible and make it real to you. Once this happens you will have Almighty God to rely upon. For a while you might not see any changes, but God's promise stands true. Keep on going and believing God. He is faithful to keep His promises.

One of the assistant pastors of my church rested in God's promise to provide the necessities in life, and found an unusual source of provision.

When the communists invaded South Korea they tried to destroy Christianity, wantonly killing 500 ministers and destroying 2,000 churches. Many of the ministers tried to flee. But this one preacher chose to stay, desiring to continue to care for his congregation. During the daytime he hid in the mountains; in the evenings he returned to the town to preach and pastor.

One winter day, however, it snowed so much that he lost his way. He searched for the path to the town, but was lost. By evening he was cold, hungry, and exhausted. Still, he could not find the way to his town. So he knelt in the snow, and prayed: "Lord Jesus, my life and death are dependent upon you. I am putting myself into your hands. I believe in your promise to keep and sustain me.

"I can't help but lay down in the snow and sleep. Please cover me with a blanket and watch over me throughout the night."

Then he slept. In the morning he awoke, warm and comfortable. When he opened his eyes, he found that a large tiger had come and slept against him the entire night. The tiger began to lick his face but he was not afraid. He was full of the Holy Spirit and the power of

God's promise. That large tiger had become more like a small pet cat.

While passing through a tempestuous storm with the wind shrieking around the ship, the waves rising to mountainous proportions, the ship rolling about like a poorly made toy, with the people on board completely devoid of hope—even then Paul stood and declared that he belonged to God. Even then Paul declared that he served God. Even then Paul declared his trust in a promise. Through these three faith confessions, the secrets to surmounting the storms of difficulty, Paul was immovable.

Let us also be assured that we belong to God through faith in Christ. If you are uncertain, you are of all people most miserable. Change that attitude now by asking Christ to be your Savior, and God to be your Father.

Let us also serve God. If you have put your trust in things of your own earthly desire, know they will fail you. May Christ be your Lord as well as your Savior. Put your trust in the eternal God who never fails you.

Let us also place our hope in God's promises. Read the Bible often, and let the Holy Spirit make specific promises alive to you. Declare those promises boldly, and you will pass through your storm of difficulty like Paul, with everyone escaping safely ashore! (Acts 27:44, TLB).

11

Experiencing God Daily

A few years ago I was traveling abroad to speak in various countries. In one country I preached on nearly thirty occasions to groups involving a total of more than 25,000 people. Although some of those meetings had lasting spiritual results, I became greatly troubled by the condition of the majority of churches in that country.

There were many beautiful churches but every Sunday most were nearly empty. Even the Christians who attended church seemed restless and rootless, more like a collection of orphans than a family of believers.

Those believers were often good people. But their knowledge of what God intended for their lives was limited, and their joy even less. They had ceased allowing Christ to be alive and vibrant in their day-to-day encounters. They had lost sight of the need to experience God daily.

Since God was not a vibrant reality in their daily lives, all problems seemed greater. They were not continually tuned into the voice that gave them correct direction. They lit their Christian lives with a forty-watt bulb, when God's power plant would have supplied enough electricity to brightly light their entire world. And such is sometimes the case with each of us.

Christ's Provision: Grace That Makes Us Beautiful

We Christians have often heard about the grace of Jesus Christ. This phrase was alive to us in the beginning of our lives as believers. Though still pleasing to the ear, for most it has become just another theological phrase.

In the Greek language grace is *karis*. When older Greek people see beautiful scenery, like a tall and lush mountain flowing with clear streams, they say *karis*. When they hear music of a beauty that captures the mind, taking it to heights of delight, they say *karis*. *Karis* refers to a special element in the beauty of nature, fine art and music, and the beautiful actions of human beings.

Grace is provided through Christ's life on earth and His death on the cross. Through accepting His grace in faith, Christ comes to you and makes you a creature of beauty. He changes your character, and as you allow Him, develops a beautiful, new personality in you. He can make your home beautiful. He can make your life beautiful.

In the Bible we read of "the richness of God's free grace lavished upon us" (Eph. 1:7, NEB). This is a grace not to be experienced just once in your life, but at many points.

About twenty years ago my mother-in-law and I visited one of the worst homes we had ever seen. This family's house was filled with ten children, but was empty of material possessions. The husband and father of that house was an alcoholic.

This man had been addicted to narcotics at one time as well. His nephew was president of the leading medical college in Korea, and had tried everything to cure his uncle from addiction, but had failed. He then encouraged his uncle to modify his habit, and switch from narcotics to alcohol.

This switch, however, brought a worse change. His uncle, father of the ten children, eventually became a chronic alcoholic. He drank liquor from early in the morning until late in the evening.

All his sons shined shoes to try to make enough money to support the family. But their father took any money they made, buying liquor instead of food. The money the father made was also used for his alcohol. With no finances, his entire family lived like beggars.

When I talked to his wife about life in Jesus Christ she was dejected. She was thin from malnutrition. She had heart trouble and stomach pains, her mental state one of deep depression. She did not want to listen to me when I talked to her.

"I want to die," she responded. "The best thing that could happen to me is death. But because of my love for my family, I won't commit suicide. Sir, be kind to me. Won't you please kill me?"

"I didn't come here to kill you," I said firmly. "I came here to tell you about the grace of Jesus Christ."

"But I don't care about going to heaven," she replied. "I am not worried about hell. I have already been living in hell for a long time."

"Sister," I challenged her, "would you like to see your life changed? Would you like to see your husband changed? Would you like to see Christ come into your house and make your home a place of beauty?"

"Oh, that can't be possible!" she exclaimed.

"It is," I retorted. "Jesus Christ came to give you His grace, a gift which you don't have to earn or pay for. He said His grace would be enough to meet every need. Christianity is more than good teachings, more than a religion. When you become a Christian Jesus Christ comes into your life. He gives you His grace. He makes you beautiful."

She listened with interest to my words, and started attending my church. Soon she was lifted from her depression. God healed her stomach pains and heart trouble. She decided to be a Christian, and became a beautiful person. Her entire personality was changed by the power of Christ. From that time on my mother-in-law and I prayed with her for her husband to be delivered from alcoholism.

Everybody who heard that we were praying for her husband laughed at us. Many times he would come to church himself, just to ridicule us. Yet we were persistent in our prayers to God. We knew the grace of Jesus Christ could change his desires and personality.

A few months passed. One morning I got up at four o'clock for our daily early morning prayer meeting. After preaching to the people, we all began to pray.

Suddenly I felt as if I were falling into a deep sleep. It seemed as if my spirit was lifted up, and I could see the glory of heaven. Then Christ's voice spoke to my heart: *"My son, I have heard your prayers."*

I was full of joy. I rushed to my mother-in-law, saying, "Mother, Jesus has heard our prayers."

Later, while eating breakfast, one of the sons of the alcoholic came to my house. In his hand was a message: his father was dying. I was astounded! Just that morning Christ had given me the assurance he was going to be well.

So my mother-in-law and I rushed to their home. There we found the man near death. His wife sadly told us, "All night he has been screaming and dying, threatening to kill all of us."

As I watched him screaming I could sense something else. He was not really dying. Satan, however, had a firm grasp on his life and mind, harassing him to think and act as if death were a soon reality.

So we banded together and prayed, rebuking the spirit of Satan. We claimed victory in the name of the Lord Jesus Christ. We could then feel the beautiful presence of the Lord.

Instantly the man fell into a deep sleep. We left the house believing, praising God for victory. Jesus had touched that alcoholic with His grace. Since that time he has never had another drop of alcohol. God's grace began to help change him into a different person.

His friends started to help him. One friend gave his family a sack of rice, and the father brought it home instead of selling it for liquor. It was the first time he had brought rice to his home in ten years. His wife was so moved that she started crying.

She then remembered my sermon on paying tithes. So she took out one-tenth of the rice, but felt uneasy about giving it to God. "Now, Jesus," she argued, "you know we need this rice. You will understand if we don't give tithes on this rice."

So she poured the tenth of the rice back. Then she again remembered God's principle of tithing, and again took out one-tenth. After a while she poured the rice back again. The struggle inside her was great.

But at four o'clock the next morning, with great courage, she took the one-tenth of rice again. She left her home, and started on the way to church. While she walked, tears flooded her eyes. Not being able to see the road clearly, she stumbled and fell in the dirt many times. She finally arrived for early morning prayers, filthy and forlorn. She handed me the rice, fell to the floor, and cried. She looked so sad that I wanted to give the rice back to her. But I did not. She had to learn the basics of the Christian life. She had to learn how to experience Christ's grace daily. So we prayed together, and I blessed her in the name of Jesus.

One month later she came running to our house. "Pastor, pastor," she exclaimed, "a miracle has happened!"

"What happened?" I asked.

She responded with excitement, "We have been eating out of that one sack of rice for more than a month! This morning my husband asked me how I was managing to feed the family with only one sack of rice. But it has lasted for more than one month!"

We went to her house to look at the rice. There was exactly one-tenth, the amount of their tithe, remaining in the sack. Every time she took out some rice to cook, one-tenth had always remained. It was a miracle that continued until her husband bought another sack of rice. As soon as he bought another sack of rice, the first sack became empty.

Christ's daily grace also began to work in their home. Because of their poverty, all the children worked hard the entire day. But then the children started going to school.

The husband is presently an elder of the church. Two of the children are now ministers, each with homes filled with the beauty of lives committed to

Christ. That entire family had learned the importance of experiencing Christ's grace daily.

God's Care: Love to Live By

There are four words in the Greek lanugage to express different kinds of love. One word is *eros*. This is the kind of love one feels for the opposite sex.

I love my wife very much, and she loves me. While away on evangelistic trips abroad I try to write her a letter every day. However, I can sense some egotistical feelings in our love, for there are times I want her to love me even more than I love her. There are times she wants to receive more love than she gives. So occasionally we have arguments, arguments that spring from a struggle for power, rather than a stability in selfless love.

I have been in the ministry for more than two decades. During this period I have counseled with many couples having trouble in their marriages. Most of these problems were caused by self-centered, egotistical love. God's love is different. His is not the egotistical, *eros* love.

Another Greek word for love is *phileo*. This is the type of love between friends. Love between friends is less egotistical, but there are still restrictions. While you have abundance in your life and prosperity in your business you will have many friends. But once you encounter failure in business or other deep difficulties, many of your friends, one by one, will leave you. *Phileo* love also fails in the face of surmounting problems.

Storge is a third Greek word for love. This is the love between parents and their children. This kind of love involves a different type of commitment.

During the Korean War many people went to Busan, in Korea's far south. Most people living in Busan, my home then, were very poor, living from day to day. There were not even any jobs to be found.

Because we were desperate for food, we even stole. When American soldiers started hauling coal by freight train from Busan's harbor, many young boys like myself would climb into the filled freight cars like hungry ants. We stole enough coal to sell, wanting to buy enough food and clothes to make it through a small portion of the harsh winter.

One day a group of refugees climbed up on a cargo train to steal coal. Then an American military policeman came running toward them, shouting for them to get down. Frightened, they jumped out of the cargo train.

One small seven-year-old boy was among the group fleeing. He started to run with the rest of the group when he saw some coal that had fallen under the train. He crawled under the train to retrieve that coal. Just as he was about to reach the coal, the train began to move. The people standing nearby shrieked, but no one dared to save that boy and endanger their own lives.

Then one middle-aged man ran near the train. With a burst of his full strength he pushed the boy to safety, clear of the railroad tracks. But the man was no longer safe. In the next moment we heard the cracking of this man's bones as the train's steel wheels tore his body apart. That man had given his life for the young boy. That man was the young boy's father.

Such is the love of caring parents. *Storge* love spurs parents to actions of brave concern. It is a wonderful kind of love. But it, too, has limitations. It is a love limited to parents and their children.

In the Greek language the love of God is *agape*. *Agape* is different from *eros*, different from *phileo*, and different from *storge*. *Agape* is unconditional love, the love of God shown through Christ's life, and through His death on the cross of Calvary.

God does not love us because we can give Him something in return. He does not love us because we can share congenial times of friendship. He does not love us because we have reached some human point of perfection. God loves us without condition. God is love, and it is His nature to love.

Christ lived a sinless life and willingly died the torturous death of a criminal because of His *agape* love. Christ died the death that we should have died on the cross. Through Christ God proved that He loved us— you and me—in spite of our sins, in spite of our weaknesses, in spite of the fact that we do not deserve His love.

By placing your faith in God, He can cleanse you of your sins and grant you His forgiveness. With Jesus' resurrection God's power was proven, power that can undergird your weaknesses.

God gives an invitation to us all: "Come to me, all whose work is hard, whose load is heavy; and I will give you relief" (Matt. 11:28, NEB). God's love is love for today, a love that you and I can live by.

Never doubt that you are deeply loved by God. You have the ability and privilege to speak directly to God. Do not worry about your past sins; God can grant you forgiveness through faith in Christ. Do not worry about your failures; God can give you the strength to overcome and succeed. Do not worry about your inadequacies; through Christ you are made strong. Do not worry about your frustrations; God has shown the ultimate frustration, death, to be powerless when He purposes.

Much of the Bible is an account of God's love to man. Read it daily, and let it speak of God's love to you. Make prayer a part of your daily activities. Talk to God honestly from the depths of your heart and mind. And let God answer you with words of love and wisdom.

You are deeply loved by God.

The Role of the Holy Spirit

In his second letter to the believers in Corinth, Paul closed with these words: "The grace of the Lord Jesus Christ, and the love of God, and fellowship in the Holy Spirit, be with you all" (2 Cor. 13:14, NEB). In these words the Apostle Paul recognized the importance of experiencing the grace of Christ and the love of God. He also points out a third aspect: the presence of the

Holy Spirit. If this verse were paraphrased directly from the Greek language, it would read: "Let the grace of Jesus Christ, and the love of God, be in you *through* the fellowship of the Holy Spirit." The Holy Spirit is the means through which we receive the grace of Jesus and the love of God.

The Greek word for fellowship in this verse is *koinonia*. *Koinonia* means "fellowship," a fellowship involving three crucial aspects.

Fidelity in Fellowship

The era of the Old Testament days was primarily the time when our heavenly Father himself dealt with man, more directly than in times since. Then the Father sent His Son, and Christ lived and walked among man for thirty-three years.

While alive on earth Christ told of another who would follow Him: "I will ask the Father and he will give you another Comforter, and he (that Comforter) will never leave you . . . when the Father sends the Comforter instead of me—and by the Comforter I mean the Holy Spirit—he will teach you much, as well as remind you of everything I myself have told you" (John 14:16, 26, TLB).

Now, through the person of the Holy Spirit, we can experience God's love and Christ's grace. The Holy Spirit is a person, the third member of the triune God.

You cannot truly know a person just by his name, nor even through a formal introduction and the polite exchange of greetings. You only know a person through intimate fellowship and the sharing of mutual love. To have fellowship with another person you must understand one another, talk with one another, share ideas, fears, dreams and hopes. To experience God daily you must have this kind of fellowship with the Holy Spirit. You must welcome Him into your heart, talk to Him sincerely, and appreciate His presence.

Many famous theological seminaries have sent their students to talk with me. They want to find the secret of my ministry's success. My reply to them has been: "I have this success because of the Holy Spirit.

"It is important to recognize and appreciate the presence of the Holy Spirit. Whenever I go up to the platform to preach, I pray: 'Dear Holy Spirit, guide my thoughts, and bless the words I speak.' Then I pray, 'Dear Holy Spirit, bless many people during this service.' After I preach I pray, 'Dear Holy Spirit, thank you for your precious power.' When I am reading the Bible, I pray, 'Holy Spirit, enlighten my heart. Teach me. Let me know the truths of God.' "

Welcome the Holy Spirit in the daily activities of your life, no matter how unimportant they seem. Depend on the Holy Spirit, and tell Him you appreciate Him. This is when fellowship with the Holy Spirit truly begins. Remember: "He will never leave you" (John 14:16, TLB).

Power of Partnership

Koinonia also means partnership. Without the Holy Spirit as our partner we can never accomplish anything great for God.

This is one of the main reasons why many churches are becoming empty. This is one reason why many young people are leaving the church. Without the Holy Spirit the Kingdom of God cannot be properly built, and we cannot experience the grace of Jesus or the love of God.

When I go to foreign countries with a language I do not know, I have to use an interpreter to communicate. I speak in English, and the interpreter translates the thoughts in my words into his native language. In a sense we are partners. If this partnership is good, the service will be a success. If our partnership is ever broken, the people listening will not understand, and the service will be a failure.

Have you ever wondered why there have been spiritual failures in your Christian life? Do you wonder why there is little success in your prayer life? Do you know why miracles do not abound in your Christian walk? It is because you have failed to have a proper day-to-day partnership with the Holy Spirit. But when you sincerely invite the Holy Spirit to come, He establishes a supernatural partnership with you. You are then in a partnership for the business of building up the Kingdom of God. The Holy Spirit becomes your senior partner. You become the junior partner. If you do not listen to your senior partner you will fail in building the Kingdom of God.

You must ask the Holy Spirit to be your senior partner. He has been with you, but He has been neglected. He has been mistreated. You must welcome Him, and enter into your Christian life with the Holy Spirit as your senior partner. He will pray through you. He will live in you and do business with you, making your life a success.

The Holy Spirit wants to build the Kingdom of God through you. He wants to give you the power of God that only a deepening partnership with Him can develop.

Delight in Delivery

Koinonia implies transportation. Transportation is a service we all need. When you want to go to another country, you usually go by plane, train or car. Even in supermarkets we see some of the results of transportation: the food and vegetables there have been transported from places hundreds of miles away. And the transportation of these goods enriches our lives.

Most of us remember a person who brought us many things we wanted and needed: the deliveryman. He brought us everything from food, to television sets, to furniture. Though we usually ignored his importance, he brought things to us that made our living more enjoyable.

In a sense the Holy Spirit is God's delivery person.

The Holy Spirit transports the grace of Jesus Christ and the love of God from God's heavenly throne to your heart, to your home, and to your church. The Holy Spirit also transports your prayers to the throne of God.

The Spirit of God is constantly moving between God and you. The Holy Spirit is God's gift to you, responsible to deliver to those with faith all God's good gifts, responsible to answer all prayers based on God's guidance. And He delights in His responsibilities, for it is His desire to follow the Father's every command.

For a potent Christian life, you need to experience God daily. Jesus Christ has provided you with grace that makes you beautiful. In God's tender care He has given you love to live by. Through fellowship with the Holy Spirit, Christ's grace and God's love can be yours. Make the Holy Spirit your senior partner, and let the power, grace, and love of God flow freely in your life. Experience God daily and let the vibrancy of that experience radiate to all around you!